COPYRIGHT

GW00514890

LIMITATION OF LIABILITY

Introduction To IT Principles

Before working through this *IT Principles* resource pack it is important that you read the following information that has been written to offer you guidance on how to get the best out of this resource pack.

The resource pack has been divided into units. Each unit consists of a number of related categories. Throughout these categories are tasks, designed to help you understand how to use the computer and how the different parts of a computer work.

At your own pace, you are required to read through the resource pack, learning about different aspects of the computer and how it is used to help understand the important and basic principles of Information Technology.

At key moments throughout the resource pack you will be instructed to perform a practical assignment or task. These tasks are there to demonstrate with a practical hands-on approach, the important theoretical aspects of the computer that might otherwise be difficult to understand merely by reading through the resource pack.

Some of the topics of this resource pack are required for specific qualifications, you may need to consult the relevant resource pack 1 to achieve the qualification aims.

By following these simple instructions and correctly using this resource pack, you will find that learning about IT Principles will be far easier and much more enjoyable.

Contents

File Management Within My Computer

Finding Files

Viewing Printer Settings

Software Applications

Integrated Applications

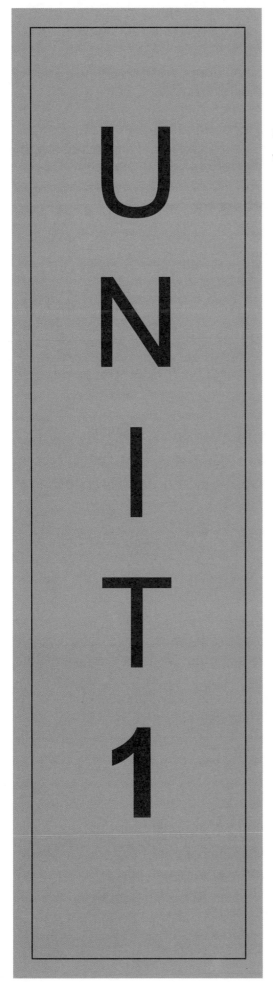

On completion of this unit, you will have learnt about:

Computer Hardware

- Input Devices
- Output Devices
- Installing Input/Output Devices

Printers

- Selecting An Alternative Printer

Advanced Display Systems

- Resolution
- What is VGA?
- SVGA
- XGA
- Refresh Rate

Media/Storage Devices

- Hard Disk Drive (HDD)
- Floppy Disks
- Zip Drives
- CD-ROM/RW
- Data Cartridge
- Memory Storage Device Comparisons
- Data Storage Table
- Computer Performance And Efficiency

Computer Hardware

The main components that make up your average computer come in a variety of shapes and sizes with differing specifications for performing different tasks.

In essence, most of the software applications used for general office duties at work, for leisure and for entertainment pursuits at home can more than easily be accommodated by your average PC.

PC hardware generally consists of the following pieces of equipment:

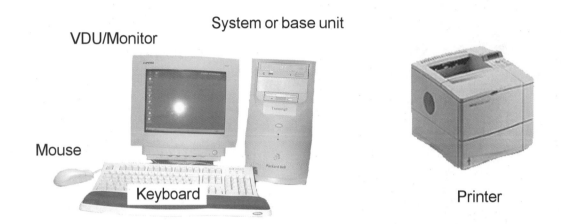

VDU/Monitor   System or base unit

Mouse

Keyboard   Printer

Most speakers are now incorporated into the design of the monitor, usually appearing at each side of it.

Computer components can then be broken down further into the categories of input and output devices.

Input Devices

As its name might suggest, an input device is a piece of hardware that allows you to communicate an instruction or an item of data to the computer. A good example is your keyboard. This is an input device because you are telling the computer, via the keys, exactly what it is you wish to say. Your data is then processed by the base unit and the information displayed through an output device, ie a monitor.

Other input devices include:

Mouse/pointer device

A mouse is a pointing device that enables you to interact with the computer via the monitor. You are able to move the mouse pointer over the screen by moving the mouse in the direction you want to go. This causes the roller ball under the mouse to rub against sensors, which transfer the movement to the mouse pointer on the screen. You can select items on the screen by clicking with one of the mouse buttons. The mouse pointer can take on different shapes according to where and what it is hovering over.

Tracker ball

A tracker ball is similar to a mouse with the exception that it has a large ball on top that is moved to control a pointer on the screen. A tracker ball can be controlled by the fingers or by the palm of the hand, making it useful to individuals who have difficulty using the mouse through physical impairment.

Joystick

A joystick is a pointing device that controls movement on the screen. It comes in the shape of a long stick attached to a plastic base with control buttons programmed for use, usually in conjunction with computer games.

Touch pad

A touch pad is another alternative to a mouse as it also interacts with a pointer on the screen. It works by sensing the movement of a finger exerting a downward pressure on the touch pad. Touch pads can be found on most laptop computers.

Touch screen

Almost simultaneously an input and output device, this piece of equipment enables you to communicate with the computer by touching the screen. Touch screens most popularly appear in the shape of kiosks and lightweight plasma screens, allowing for a dynamic interactive digital workboard.

Scanner

A scanner is an input device that converts printed text or images into electrical signals that the computer can understand. They are widely used to input large quantities of previously typed text. Scanners can either be flatbed or hand-held. Flatbed scanners come in a variety of sizes, the most common being A4 and they are able to scan a whole page of text or images at a time.

Light pen

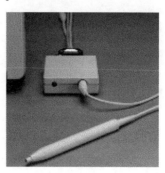

A light pen is a light-sensitive detector in the shape of a pen and is used to select objects on the monitor. Light pens are used for tasks that involve a lot of updating such as on-line forms. A light pen is also known as a light stylus. Similar technology to that used in the creation of the light pen is used at supermarket check-outs to calculate the price of groceries.

Microphone

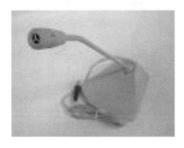

A microphone can be used to input data into a computer, either by speech or other audio sounds. The computer needs to be trained to recognise a particular speech pattern and often requires the user to spend a few hours teaching it. The advent of the Internet also means that, increasingly, microphones are being used to communicate with other users worldwide.

Digital/video cameras

Once an image or sequence of film has been captured, it can be fed into your computer and manipulated, provided you have the correct software to alter it.

Output Devices

Once a computer has processed the data it has received, it requires an output device to communicate this information to the user. Output devices display/communicate information in a variety of different forms, the most common being:

Visual Display Unit/VDU

VDUs, monitors, screens are the single most important output device for the computer. Made up of small dots of light, known as 'pixels', the number of pixels displayed is known as the 'screen resolution'. The resolution will depend on the hardware inside your computer and the monitor you have.

Monitors are available in different sizes, ranging from 12" to 42" in a diagonal measure. The larger the monitor, the higher the price. The most common sizes for monitors are 15", 17" and 21". These sizes reflect the size of the 'tube' within the monitor and not the 'viewing area', which tends to be less than the stated size.

Printers

Used to provide hard copy output, there are several different types of printer, including dot matrix, thermal, inkjet and laser.

Possibly the most common type of printer, certainly in the workplace, would be a laser printer. This is a non-impact printer that laser prints - as its name suggests - using a laser to produce an image on a rotating drum before transferring the entire image to paper. The drum is coated with an electrically charged film which has its charge changed from negative to positive where the laser light hits it. This attracts the toner powder. The paper is passed over an electrically charged wire which is then pressed against the drum, where the toner is transferred to the paper. Heat and pressure fuse the toner to the paper. A laser printer can have resolutions of 1200dpi (dots per inch) and printing speeds of anywhere between 10 and 18 pages per minute.

Plotters

Similar to printers in that they produce hard-copy outputs, plotters are also used to create drawings, particularly in engineering and architectural applications. Plotters would be classed as an input device as well as an output device. They can also use one or more different coloured pens. The computer gives instructions to the plotter so that it knows which pen to use and where on the paper to draw. Some plotters allow the paper to move on one axis and the pen on another; the less complex plotters only move the pens.

Speakers

These are output devices that produce audio format, most commonly used for music, speech and games. They are connected to the computer via a sound card that digitally produces the sound patterns. Sound cards and speakers vary in quality and cost. Originally, speakers were, in the main, peripheral to the computer and would need to be attached to the system unit. Today, nearly all speakers are integrated into the design of the monitor.

Speech synthesizers

Speech synthesizers are used to turn text into spoken words and vice versa and have been of great value to the visually impaired user. Programmed to pick up on the individual speech patterns of the user, speech synthesizers require the user (in the first instance) to speak clearly and slowly into the microphone, enabling the computer to process the human voice into text.

Like touch screens, speech synthesizers are almost simultaneously input/output devices, as they allow speech to be textualised and text to be verbalised.

Projection devices

Projection systems are one of the most effective visual presentation tools. In various applications - business presentations or in seminars and schools - crisp, bright images are the key to maximizing impact and conveying the message in an efficient and impressive manner.

There are a number of projection devices currently available. Included among them are the CRT (Cathode Ray Tube). This technology was used in the creation of the television set but has since been superseded by digital technology.

Digital Light Processing (DLP) was invented almost 5 years ago by a company in the US called Texas Instruments. DLP projection technology screens were originally designed to supersede CRT projection and compete with LCD (Liquid Crystal Display).

Whatever the technology involved, the main use of modern-day projection devices is in the commercial field. Companies are always looking for brighter, higher specification, portable projectors capable of replaying high resolution PC displays in high ambient light areas.

CRT technology is starting to be phased out in these applications now that DLP, LCD and their other competitors are starting to evolve. DLPs are also now being used as the projection technology in the new breed of 'Digital Cinemas' that are beginning to appear in ever increasing numbers around the world.

T A S K	1.	**Make a list of all input and output devices connected to your computer.**
	2.	**Look round the room to see what other devices are used and note these as well.**
	3.	**Keep a list of these devices in your folder.**

Installing Input/Output Devices

In order to install the essential components of the computer correctly, you need to have the appropriate leads for each device.

The main power lead has a socket or 'female' connection that attaches to the system unit, while the other end of the lead has a fused three-pin plug that fits into the power source.

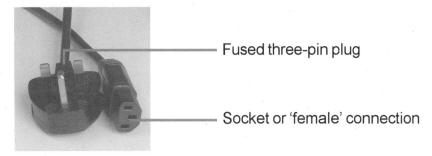

Fused three-pin plug

Socket or 'female' connection

The monitor lead has plug and socket or 'male and female' connectors at either end of the lead. The plug connection fits into the system unit while the socket is attached to the monitor. Some monitors may also have a separate power lead.

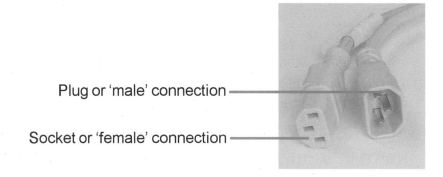

Plug or 'male' connection

Socket or 'female' connection

Typical tower unit

Situated at the back of the base unit are the connections or 'ports' for each of the components mentioned.

Mains input which connects the system unit to the power supply.

Mains output which connects to the monitor.

Ports for connection of mouse, keyboard, printer etc.

Connects System Unit to the power supply

The diagram to the right displays the system unit with leads connecting the monitor, keyboard and the mouse. The main lead connects the system unit to the power supply.

Keyboard

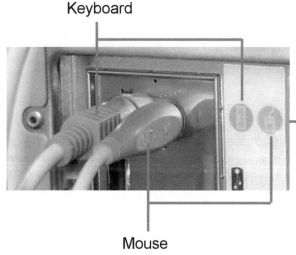

Connects monitor to System Unit

Mouse

The keyboard and mouse connectors may be colour coded and labelled with icons to help the user find the correct ports more easily.

NB Only switch the power supply on once all the other leads connecting their respective components to the system unit have been firmly secured!

Printers

All **printers** have a number of different options that allow the user to print the hard copy of a document in a variety of formats. These configurations or additional features of the document can help to alter its appearance or may enable the user to produce samples of a document both efficiently and economically.

In order to see the printer configuration, click **Start**, **Settings** and select **Printers.**

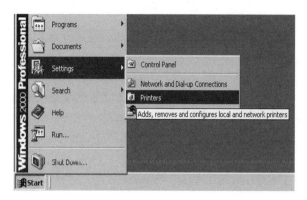

The available printers will be listed in the resulting dialogue box. The default printer will be indicated with a tick.

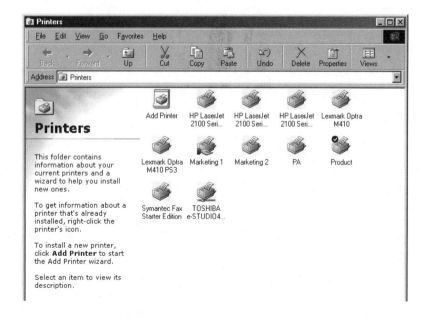

The default printer is the one from which your computer will automatically print copies of your work. To change the default printer, right-click an alternative printer and select **Set as Default** from the pop-up menu.

To view the settings of a printer, select the printer and click **File**, **Properties** from the menu bar.

Selecting An Alternative Printer

Your computer may be connected to a number of printers, allowing you to choose from a number of printers when producing hard copies of your work (this overrides the default). With a document open and ready for printing, select **File**, **Print** from the menu bar. The **Print** dialogue box will appear as shown below. Select the printer of choice from the **Name:** drop-down menu, then click **OK** to confirm.

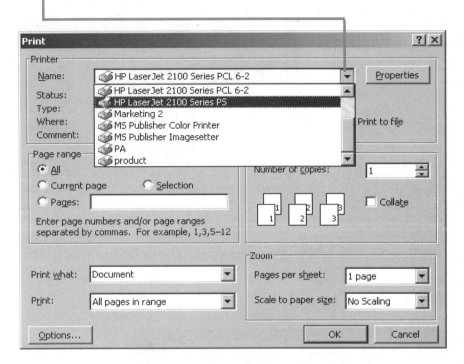

T A S K	Before you carry out this task, please check with a tutor the location and availability of the disconnected machine. Do not disconnect the computer you are currently using.
	1. You are required to put together a monitor, system unit, mouse, keyboard and connect the power cables.
	2. Please check with a tutor that all connections are correct before turning the power on.
	3. Return to your computer, ensure it is turned on and check the printers available and the name of the default printer. Note these and keep for future reference.

Advanced Display Systems

Resolution

Resolution is the number of pixels (individual points of colour) contained on a display monitor, expressed in terms of the number of pixels on the horizontal axis and the number on the vertical axis. The sharpness of the image on a display depends on the resolution and the size of the monitor. The same pixel resolution will be sharper on a smaller monitor and gradually lose sharpness on larger monitors because the same number of pixels are being spread out over a larger number of inches. A video card plays an essential role in today's PCs. The card converts digital information into information that can be displayed on the monitor.

What Is VGA?

VGA stands for Video Graphics Array. Nearly every video card has VGA compatibility - and it is fairly easy to program. It offers many different video modes, from 2 colour to 256 colour, and resolutions from 320x200 to 640x480 pixels. The most common VGA mode comprises of 256-colours and is known as mode 0x13.

In mode 0x13, the screen dimensions are 320 pixels in width and 200 pixels in height. This is mapped 0 to 319 on the x (horizontal) axis and 0 to 199 on the y (vertical) axis, with the origin (0,0) at the top-left corner (Figure 1). Since this is a 256-colour mode, each pixel represents 8 bits (2^8=256) or one byte, so the memory needed is 320*200 or 64,000 bytes.

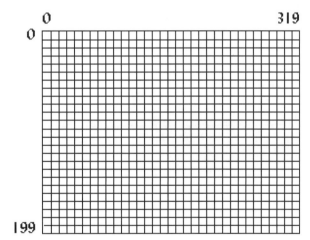

Figure 1.

SVGA

Super Video Graphics Array is a video display standard for colour monitors. SVGA monitors can display up to 16.7 million colours and resolutions up to 1,280 x 1,024 pixels. Most new computers offer SVGA - these tend to be 800x600 pixels.

SVGA is much more advanced than VGA. In most cases, one SVGA card can produce millions of colours at a choice of resolutions, but the abilities depend on the card and the manufacturer. There is currently no market standard for SVGA (therefore this is known as a 'loose term').

XGA

Following on from the SVGA display is the XGA (Extended Graphics Array).

XGA is a high-resolution video display mode that provides screen pixel resolution of 1,024 by 768 in 256 colours or 640 by 480 in high (16-bit) colour. XGA monitors can be interlaced displays (interlaced being a term associated with images used on the Internet).

XGA-2 is a display mode that provides 1,024 by 768 resolution in high colour and higher refresh rates than XGA. XGA was introduced by IBM in 1990 as an improvement on an earlier IBM display standard. The XGA standard is used in desktop and laptop computers as well as in projection systems.

Refresh Frequency

The refresh frequency (number of frames scanned per second) varies, but it is normally between 60 and 100 hertz. Refresh frequencies slower than 60 Hz produce distracting screen flicker, which can cause headaches and eye fatigue.

To view the refresh frequency in the Windows 2000 operating environment, click **Start**, **Settings**, **Control Panel** then double-click the **Display** icon. Select the **Settings** tab, click **Advanced**, select the **Monitor** tab; the **Refresh Frequency** is shown here.

T A S K	1.	Find the refresh rate of the computer monitor that you are working on.

Media/Storage Devices

Data storage is an essential part of producing work (any kind of work) on a computer. Saving your work to a storage device other than one built in to the computer: (a) ensures that your work is safe in the eventuality of the computer crashing (b) means your work can be used on another computer (c) means you do not store work on the hard drive unnecessarily.

There are many storage devices on the market that will enable you to store work for access at a later date.

Hard Disk Drive (HDD)

The hard drive is the main storage medium in PCs and is usually permanently installed inside the computer. Hard drives can transfer data quickly and have large storage capacities amounting to several gigabytes.

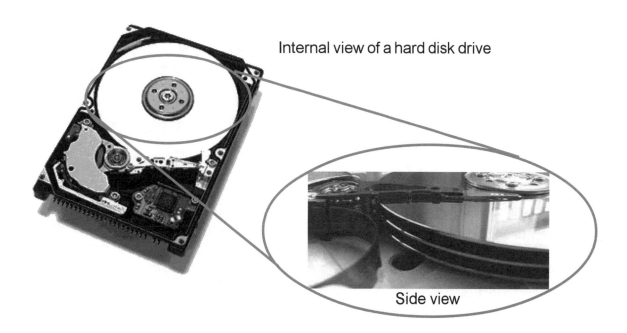

Internal view of a hard disk drive

Side view

Hard disk drives are made up of rigid platters composed of either aluminium alloy or a mixture of glass and ceramic. Both sides of the platters are coated with a magnetic medium. Typically, two or three platters are stacked on top of each other with a common spindle that turns the whole assembly at several thousand revolutions per minute. Data is recorded onto the magnetic surface. This is commonly known as a mass storage device, holding anywhere between one hundred megabytes and several gigabytes of information.

The operating system and most of the other software applications on the computer are installed on the hard drive. You can also store files and documents that you work with on it. If your computer is connected to a network, you may also be able to store data on the network server hard drive.

Floppy Disks

Floppy disks are often referred to as diskettes. They are small removable units used in disk drives usually referred to as the A: drive. Nowadays, diskettes are 3½" in size and have a hard plastic protective case with a metal or plastic cover that slides back when inserted in the disk drive, exposing the magnetic coated disk. Floppy disks are usually high-density double-sided disks with a storage capacity of 1.44Mb. Double density disks have a storage capacity of 720Kb. Floppy disks need to be formatted prior to use, although pre-formatted disks are available. Formatting prepares the disk for the type of computer it is to be used in, such as Apple Mac or IBM-compatible PC.

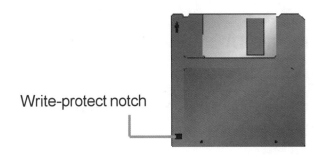

Write-protect notch

Floppy disks can be protected from being over-written by a write-protect notch that slides across one of the small holes in the disk. Floppy disks require a great deal of care to ensure they are not damaged and the information held on them lost.

They should be kept away from all magnetic sources and heat sources, and should be stored carefully in boxes or other dust-free environments. You should not slide back the metal cover and do not touch the magnetic surface.

Floppy disks are a cheap storage medium with a relatively small storage capacity.

Zip Drives

A zip disk is a removable disk that is capable of storing 100Mb or more of information. Zip disks look like floppy disks and the drives can be internal or external to the computer. They are very fast and are used to keep back up copies of data files. They are also useful when transferring files from one computer to another. However, these disks are expensive in comparison to floppy disks.

CD-ROM/RW

A **CD-ROM (Compact Disk Read-Only Memory)** disk is a round disk resembling an audio CD. Software is usually distributed on CD-ROM and the information is burned onto the surface of the disk. A laser beam in the drive unit reads this information. CD-ROMs have a large capacity, typically 650Mb (which is more than 500 floppy disks). They are cheap and extremely reliable.

A **CD-R** is a recordable CD-ROM that can be written to only once. A **CD-RW** is a recordable CD that can be written to many times. A CD-rewriter drive can be external or internal and although it is often separate from the CD-ROM drive, in many new machines one drive can be used for both purposes.

Data Cartridge

This form of data storage is also known as 'magnetic tape' and is slower and cheaper than other magnetic storage devices. It is used mainly for backing up data in large organisations. It is very reliable. The consequence of using magnetic tape means that data has to be read sequentially from start to finish until the required information is located. Files cannot be immediately accessed as they can from disks, which use random access to locate the required data. The drives used in PCs for this storage medium are often referred to as tape-streamers.

Your machine will probably have drives A:, C: and D: (the CD-ROM drive is usually assigned the last letter to be used). If the machine has a CD-writer installed as well, this will usually be drive D: and the CD-ROM drive will become drive E:.

T A S K	1.	**Using Windows Explorer or My Computer, look at the structure of the drives on the computer you are using. Note down the names of the drives.**

Further on in the resource pack you will see how to find out what system settings and devices are available on the machine you are using.

Memory Storage Device Comparisons

	Speed - 1 being the fastest	Typical Cost	Typical Capacity
Hard Disk	1	from £60 to £2000	128 Gb
CD ROM	2	50 pence	650 Mb
Zip Disk	3	£6	100 Mb
Data Cartridge	4	£15	160 Mb
Floppy Disk	5	20 pence	1.44 Mb

Please note that all these values are subject to change due to the continuous growth of IT. Check computer magazines and catalogues for up-to-date details.

Data Storage Table

Storage Medium	Surface Abrasion	Magnetic Fields	Electrostatic Discharge	Temperature Below 0°C or Above 60°C	Humidity Below 8% or Above 90%	Physical Damage
Floppy Disk	Data loss if disk surface area exposed	Susceptible to damage even when not actually exposed to atmosphere	Susceptible to damage even when not actually exposed to atmosphere	Disk surface may be affected and drive read/write head may not be able to identify the data	Disk surface may be affected and drive read/write head may not be able to identify the data	May be easily damaged due to thin plastic coating
Hard Disk	Disk surface area sealed within a metal case not affected	If metal casing is magnetised, data on disk contained within may be corrupted	Susceptible especially if associated electronic circuits are subjected to discharge	Relatively unaffected	Relatively unaffected	Hard disk damaged if machine moved whilst operational/ switched on
CD ROM	Much more resilient but could result in data loss where surface is scratched	Not affected by magnetic fields	Not affected by electrostatic discharge	Not affected	Not affected	Extreme damage to the disk surface area will result in data loss
Tape Cartridge	Tape normally fully exposed when not in tape drive, easily damaged if exposed to surface abrasion	Easily affected if tape exposed	Susceptible if internal tape is exposed	Operation of tape cartridge may be affected resulting in tape not moving over tape head	Operation of tape cartridge may be affected resulting in tape not moving over tape head	Casing much stronger than floppy disk, but could be damaged with extreme force or if tape exposed

Computer Performance And Efficiency

A computer's performance is determined by several factors.

The first is the type of processor that determines its speed. There are several different processors available such as Pentium, Celeron and Athlon and these all have varying clock speeds measured in Megahertz. The higher the clock speed, the faster the computer.

The second factor to affect the performance of the computer is the amount of RAM (Random Access Memory) available. The more RAM available, the less 'work' a computer has to do to access the slower storage devices such as the hard disk or CD-ROM. RAM can be upgraded from 32Mb to 64Mb, 128Mb, 256Mb etc to provide increased performance.

The third factor is the size and speed of the hard disk. The larger the hard disk, the more you will be able to store on it without having to use slow floppy disks. Hard disk access time is also important in determining the performance of a computer. The quicker the access time, the faster the data retrieval.

There are several methods you can use to check the size and type of your processor and the amount of RAM on your machine.

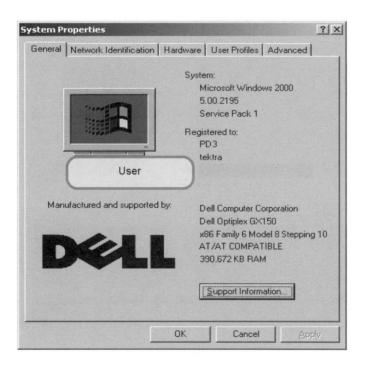

Click **Start**, **Settings**, **Control Panel**. Double-click the **System** icon.

You will then be able to see who the computer is registered to, what processor it has and how much RAM is available.

(The other options will be looked into in more detail later on in the resource pack.)

You can also open any of your Office applications, select **Help**, **About Microsoft Word** (depending on which application you are in) and then **System Info.**

This will also give you information on the processor etc.

T	1.	Using whichever method you wish, look at the system information on the computer you are using.
A		
S	2.	Note the processor and the RAM. If you use the information in the Office application, you will also be able to find the size of the processor.
K		

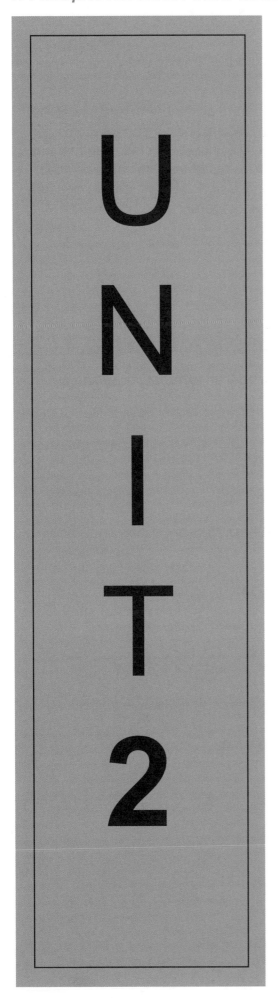

On completion of this unit, you will have learnt about:

Computers
- Workstations
- Laptops Versus PCs

Networks
- Computer Networking
- LAN (Local Area Network)
- WAN (Wide Area Network)
- Client-server Network
- Client-server Applications
- Peer-to-Peer
- Internet/Intranet
- ISPs
- URL
- Protocol

Networking
- Shared Access
- Determining Who Can Access Your Files

Desktop
- Desktop Shortcuts
- Desktop Configuration
- Date And Time
- Regional Settings
- System Tools
- Disk Defragmentation
- Disk Cleanup

Computers

Workstations

A modern and ergonomically sound working environment at the office or at home constitutes an efficient and comfortable computer workstation. Whether PC or Macintosh, a static, permanent working environment that includes peripheral hardware devices - eg printer, CD writer - represents a workstation. This is opposed to a laptop computer that has a temporary working environment and is mobile.

Laptops Versus PCs

PCs usually have bigger monitors and larger hard disk space.
PCs are static and tend to be used in one area.
Laptops are portable and can be used anywhere without an external power source.

Networks

Computer Networking

There are two types of information network, Local Area Network (LAN) and Wide Area Network (WAN).

Advantages of networking computers together include:

- Shared resources; one printer can be shared amongst many computers.
- Shared files; data can be regularly updated in one central place.
- User groups can be created; access levels can be set for increased security.
- Information/data can be backed up (copied) in one central place regularly.

Disadvantages of networking computers together include:

- Needs expert installation.
- Reliance on the networked machine (or server); this may mean that if the machine malfunctions, shared resources may not work.

LAN (Local Area Network)

A LAN is a network which connects computers and peripherals within a room, building or other locally confined area. LANs usually have cables that connect computers together. A local area network that uses high frequency radio waves or infrared beams is known as a Local Area Wireless Network (LAWN).

Each user has their own PC and, on switching on the computer, will be faced with a 'log on' screen requesting security information such as a username and password. On entering this information into the computer, the system will either accept or decline the information. A full list of users and passwords will be held on the system to eliminate unauthorised access to information held.

The network may have a 'server' which is a high specification computer used to store all information/data created and saved by users. Users will only be able to access this information if their log on credentials are accepted.

WAN (Wide Area Network)

A WAN spans a large geographic area, such as a state, province or country. WANs often connect multiple smaller networks, such as LANs.

The most popular WAN in the world today is the World Wide Web. Many smaller portions of the Internet, such as extranets, are also WANs.

WANs generally utilise different and much more expensive networking equipment than LANs.

Client-server Network

A server is the main computer in the network. The server will either be a powerful PC or mini-computer. A network operating system must be installed on the server. The other computers (or workstations) connected to the server are known as clients. A computer must also have a network adapter installed to be able to receive and send information across the network. This adapter is attached to a network cable that connects the various computers to each other.

The server provides access to shared resources, such as documents, programs, storage space, printers and scanners. This means that the clients can share both files and peripheral devices. Client-server networks can be used by almost any number of users.

A client-server network is normally managed by one or more network administrator that will help to ensure a high level of security.

Client-server Applications

Some of the most popular applications on the Internet follow the client/server design:

- e-mail clients
- FTP (File Transfer Protocol) clients
- Web browsers

Each of these programs presents a user interface (either graphic or text-based) in a client process that allows the user to connect to servers.

Peer-to-Peer

Peer-to-peer (P2P) networks eliminate the need for servers and allow all computers to communicate and share resources as peers.

Peer-to-peer can best be described as a network in which each workstation has equivalent capabilities and responsibilities. This differs from client-server architecture, in which some computers are dedicated to serving the others.

Peer-to-peer networks are a cheaper option than client server networks, since a powerful server is not required. The drawback it that security is not so tight, as individual users are responsible for the resources on their own machines.

Internet/Intranet

The **Internet** is a system of computers connected together to allow your computer to exchange data, transfer files and communicate messages with other computers also connected to the Internet.

In broad terms, it is a global collection of interconnected computers transferring information via high-speed networking connections and telephone lines.

Intranets offer private network access to company employees and other workgroups. As a private LAN designed for use by everyone within an organisation, a very simple intranet might consist of an internal e-mail system or a message board. More sophisticated intranets include one or more web site portals that contain company news, forms and personnel information.

ISPs

An **ISP** (Internet Service Provider) is a company that provides Internet connectivity to home and business customers. ISPs choose what forms of access to provide customers, ranging from traditional modem dial-up to DSL (Digital Subscriber Lines).

Recently, ISP companies have begun to diversify and offer additional services. These include e-mail, web site and database hosting and web site development services and tools. Some well-known ISPs include BT, AOL, MSN, Compuserve etc.

URL

Web sites often have links to other web pages, either on their own web site or linking to other web sites. These links are known as **Hyperlinks** and contain the addresses for the web page. These addresses are known as URLs (Uniform Resource Locators) and are unique to each web page.

URLs essentially consist of three sections:

www.bbc.co.uk

1. network protocol
2. host name or address
3. file location

The network protocol determines the underlying Internet protocol to be used in reaching the location. This consists of a standard protocol name followed by the :// characters. Typical protocols found in URLs include http://, ftp:// and mailto://.

The host immediately follows the network protocol. Hosts are commonly the name of the organisation who owns the web site.

Using the example above, the server will automatically guide you to the file 'index.htm', which is usually the home page of most web sites.

The file location section of the URL defines the location of a network resource, some of these are shown below:

.co	identifies what type of site the domain is: ac - higher educational institutions co - business com - commercial edu - educational gov - governmental body mil - military net - network org - non-profit organisation
.uk	identifies the country: .de - Germany .fr - France .it - Italy If you see an address that does not include the country identifier, it is likely to be an American company or an international business.

Protocol

Network protocols like HTTP (Hypertext Transfer Protocol) , TCP/IP (Internet Protocol) and SMTP (Simple Message Transfer Protocol) provide a foundation that much of the Internet is built on.

Protocols are basically a process of sequential events or instructions leading to a pre-defined outcome.

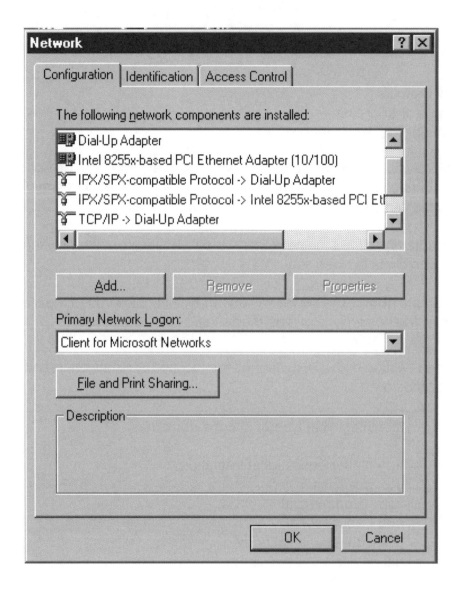

You can look at the protocols installed on your computer.

Using Windows 2000, right-click the mouse button on the **My Network Places** icon, select **Properties** from the pop-up menu. Select the **Local Area Connection** icon, right-click the mouse button and select **Properties** from the pop-up menu. A dialogue box will appear showing the protocols installed on the computer.

T
A
S
K

1. View the computer's existing protocols. Do not change any of the options. Note down information displayed.

   It is necessary to know the machine name if setting up a network, as all machines must belong to the same workgroup.

   To do this if using Windows 2000:

   Right-click the mouse button on the My Network Places icon, then select 'Properties' from the pop-up menu. Click Advanced from the menu bar, then select Network Identification.

2. Note down the computer name. You should now have a substantial list of computer properties. Keep this in your folder as reference.

Networking

Shared Access

Maintaining confidentiality and privacy over the network is important. This can be achieved by:

- closing down or logging off when absent from the computer
- not giving out your password
- setting user access (described below)

As part of a computer network in Windows 2000 you will be able to see all the computers that are on your network. However, this does not allow access to the drives on each computer. To access files you will need to enter your user name, followed by your password. This will need to be entered in the **Enter Network Password** dialogue box before you are allowed access.

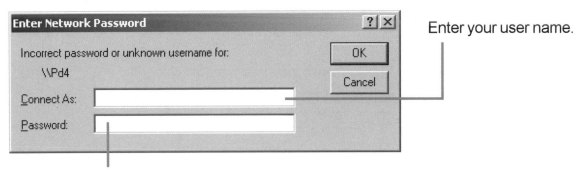

Enter your user name.

Enter your password.

Determining Who Can Access Your Files

Open the **My Computer** dialogue box on the desktop and right-click the **Local Disk (C:)**. From the pop-up menu, choose **Sharing** or right click on the **C: drive** icon using Windows Explorer.

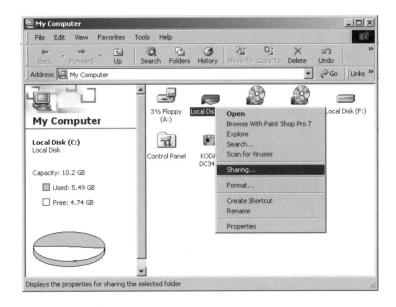

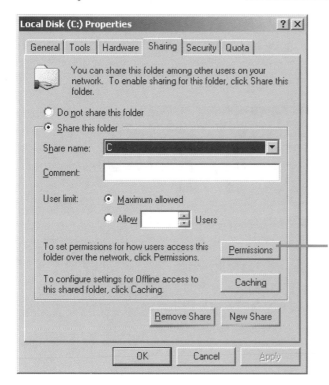

The **Permissions** button enables you to choose which computers can have access or will be restricted to the data on your computer.

The **Name** section will contain the user names of all the computers on the network with access to your computer. Use the **Add** button to select from a list of users on the network or use the **Remove** button to restrict access.

From the **Permissions** section, you can determine the degree to which users can manipulate the files on your machine.

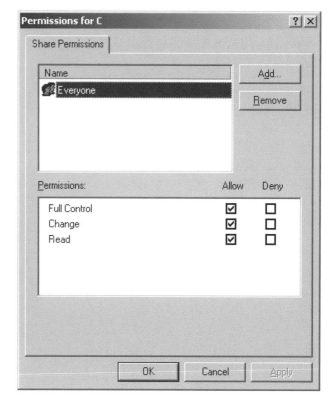

By clicking either the **Allow** or **Deny** check boxes, you can give permission for users to have **Full Control**, the capacity to **Change**, or access to simply **Read** the information on your computer.

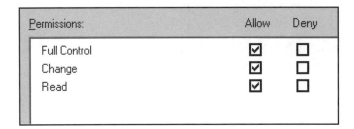

To see any other users on your network, you can do the following:

In windows 200, using Windows Explorer, go to **My Network Places**.

T A S K	1.	Using the method above for your operating system, write down if there are any other users on your network.
		Can you gain access to the drives or have they had permissions set to deny access?
	2.	Have a look at your C: drive. Does this have sharing allowed?

Desktop

Desktop Shortcuts

You can create shortcuts on the Desktop of your most commonly used software applications, to save scrolling through the Programs. Right-click the file or application icon and select **Create Shortcut** from the pop-up menu. In Windows 2000, you can also drag the icon directly onto the Desktop.

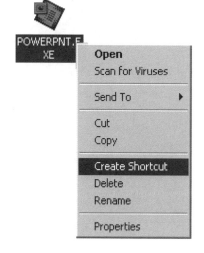

Cut and paste the Shortcut icon (distinguished by a small arrow) to the desktop.

Microsoft
PowerPoint

Desktop Configuration

Right-clicking the pointer tool over your Desktop will activate a pop-up menu from which you can select **Active Desktop**, **Customise my Desktop**. You can also use the **Start button**, **Settings**, **Control Panel**, **Display.**

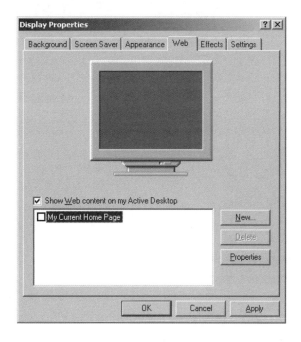

If you choose the first option, by default the **Web** tab will be selected, giving you the opportunity, via the **New** and **Properties** button, to add Internet web content to the desktop.

The **New** button provides a link via the Internet to *the Microsoft* active item desktop gallery, where you can freely download items for your desktop.

With **Properties**, you can schedule what day or time in the week to download web pages from the Internet, that can then be viewed off-line at your convenience.

If you use the second option, you will need to click the **Web** tab to show the above dialogue box.

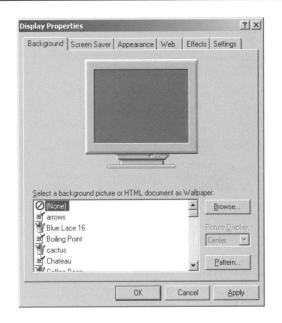

The **Background** option allows you to choose the colour or image you would like to display on the desktop.

Using the scrollbar, you can select from a list of images. Using the **Picture Display:** option provides various formats for the desktop image.

Clicking **Browse** will help you search the drives of your computer for desktop images.

Pattern will fill the active desktop space around the formatted image.

Select a **Screen Saver** using the drop-down menu and **Settings** to alter its characteristics. **Preview** will let you have a look at your choice before it is applied. With the **Wait** option you can decide how long the computer can remain inactive before the **Screen Saver** is activated.

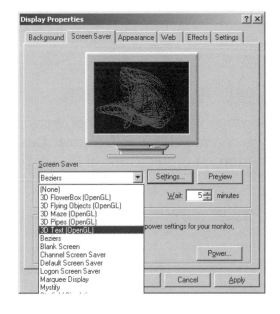

Advantages	Disadvantages
Visually appealing	Uses up computer processing power
Corporate logo can be displayed	Can become untidy within a large office
Legacy to stop phosphur burn	

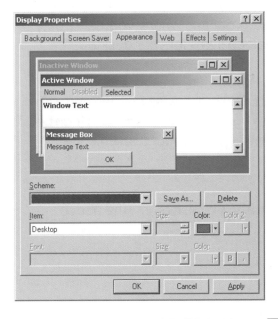

Appearance controls the colour of the windows and dialogue boxes.

You can customise the look of the Windows operating environment to your own personal taste. This includes changing the font type in the title bar of all windows and dialogue boxes.

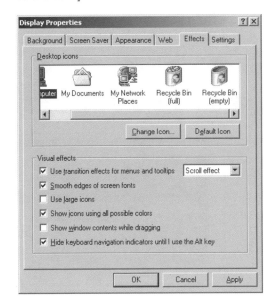

With **Effects** you can change the look and size of the icons on the Desktop and within the rest of the Windows environment that represent Drives; Files; Folders; Recycle Bin etc.

There are a number of **Visual effects** from which to choose that alter the way your icons will appear.

Having changed icons by clicking the **Change Icon** button and selecting from the available list, you can revert back to the original settings by clicking the **Default** button.

Through the **Settings** tab you have the **Colour** and **Screen area** sections. By clicking and holding the slide-handle, calibrations between **High** and **Low** will determine the amount of pixels in the screen area.

From **Colours**, you can determine the spectrum of colours used in displaying the information on the screen.

Advanced provides yet further setting options, while **Troubleshoot** gives you access to the Windows **Help** facility.

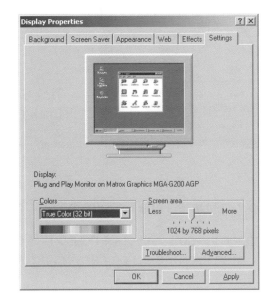

T	1.	**Note down the current desktop settings.**
A		
S	2.	**View the various desktop options. Do not make any changes to the**
K		**settings unless you are a home user.**

Date And Time

The clock is displayed on the right-hand side of the taskbar.

If the **Clock** is not displayed on the taskbar.

Click **Start**.
Click **Settings**.
Click **Taskbar & Start Menu**.

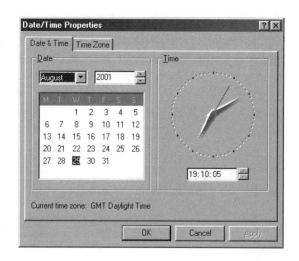

Tick **Show clock**.
Click **OK**.

To view the **Date/Time Properties** box, double-click the clock on the taskbar.

To change the hour, select the hour on the digital clock, then click the accompanying arrows to increase or decrease the value.

To change the minutes, select the minutes, then click the arrows to increase or decrease the value.

To change the seconds, select the seconds, then click the arrows to increase or decrease the value.

To change the AM/PM indicator (if your computer possesses one), select it, then click the arrows.

Click **OK** to confirm or **Cancel** to close the dialogue box without saving changes.

TASK

1. **Ensure the clock on your computer is displaying the correct time and date.**

Regional Settings

Regional settings can be altered to suit the specific user. Changes here will affect all of the applications on the computer.

To change the regional settings, click **Start**, **Settings**, **Control Panel**. Double-click the **Regional Settings** icon, the **Regional Settings Properties** dialogue box will open. Select the tabs to view the contents. Click **OK** to confirm changes.

T A S K	1.	**View the regional settings but do not make any changes.**

System Tools

System tools are applications on your computer that help to keep all your data safe, and maintain the 'smooth' operation of your computer. They also provide information on how to prevent the possibility of errors occurring within the operating system.

The applications used for the Windows 2000 operating environment are:

* Backup
* Character Map
* Disk Cleanup
* Disk Defragmentation
* Getting Started
* Scheduled Tasks
* System Information

Disk Defragmentation

Over time, files and folders on your system become fragmented, with small pieces of data being scattered over the drive that contains the file or folder.

To access the **Disk Defragmenter** dialogue box, select: **Start**
Programs
Accessories
System Tools
Disk Defragmenter.

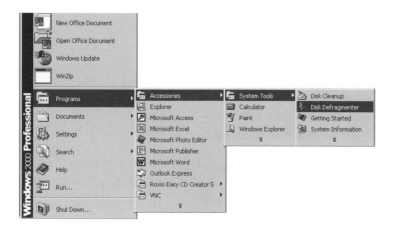

Illustration below is an example of the Windows 2000 screen.

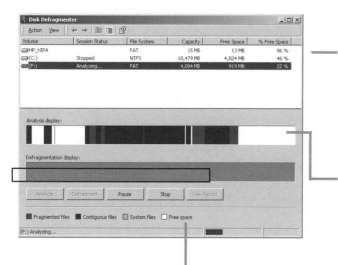

This is a table listing each drive or volume on the computer, telling you its capacity and how much free space it has available.

Once you've selected a drive from the above table, click the **Analyse** button to display the status of that drive in the **Analyse display** status bar.

Use the **colour coded legend** at the foot of the dialogue box to discern the current state of your drive.

If the drive is considered to be fine, an **Analysis Complete** dialogue box will let you know. If it is considered that defragmentation should be performed, your computer will return the following dialogue box:

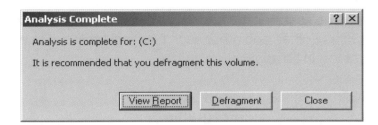

View Report will detail yet more analysis of fragmented files, while clicking **Defragment** will then set about assembling the fragmented clusters of each file/folder.

NB **Defragmentation times are dependent upon the speed of the computer's processor and the number of files to be defragmented.**

Disk Cleanup

When you access the Internet, the Internet Explorer web browser automatically downloads each page you display (including images) and saves it into the temporary files folder.

Disk cleanup helps to free space on the hard drive by searching the drive for unnecessary files, eg Temporary Files Folder, and other such files that have not been saved or are not needed to start up, or to run an application.

To cleanup a disk or drive, select: **Start**
Programs
Accessories
System Tools
Disk Cleanup.

Do not activate this option on the computer you are using.

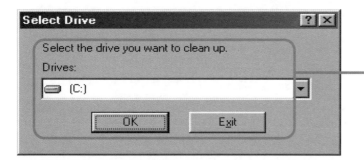

Select the drive from the drop-down menu and click **OK**.

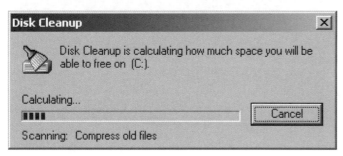

Disk Cleanup will then rapidly calculate how much space to make available on that drive.

Disk Cleanup will now have deleted all unnecessary files from the selected drive and placed them in the Recycle Bin. Clicking **View Files** will activate the **Recycle Bin** window displaying the files.

Select **Empty Recycle Bin** to permanently delete these files.

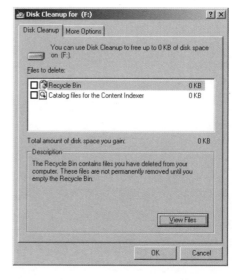

T A S K	1.	Open the dialogue box accessing the Background information of the desktop. Make a note of the Colour/Image and Pattern of your desktop.
	2.	Change all three elements and apply them to your desktop.
	3.	Return settings to their original configuration.

T A S K	1.	Access Disk Defragmenter and analyse the status of the drives on your computer.
	2.	Close the Analysis Dialogue Box.
	NB	Defragmenting your hard drive might take a considerable period of time. It is recommended that you do not defragment the drive within the centre.

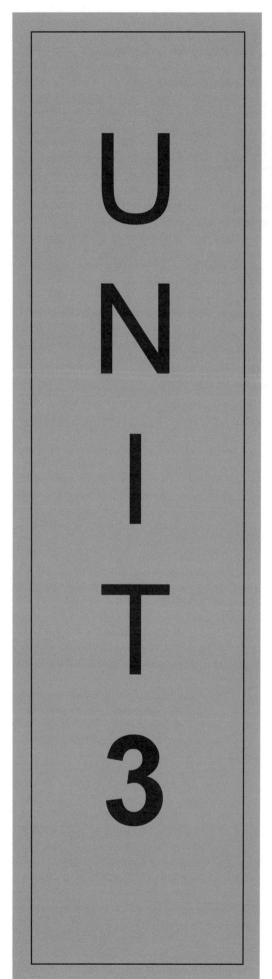

On completion of this unit you will have learnt about and practised the following:

- **Using The Operating Environment**
- Using Show/Hide Toolbars
- The Standard Toolbar
- Keyboard Shortcuts
- The Mouse/Pointer Device
- Click And Type Pointer Shapes

- **Navigating The Operating Environment**
- Using The Scroll Bars
- Using The Keyboard
- Page Magnification And Zoom
- Print Preview A Document
- Error Messages And Prompts

 ©Tektra TEKIT2RP1102

Using The Operating Environment

Using Show/Hide Toolbars

Within the Microsoft Windows operating environment, toolbars and menus are used to both edit and manipulate your work within any one of the software applications within the Microsoft Office software package.

Toolbars often contain buttons with images, menus or a combination of both. Each software application within Office includes many built-in toolbars that you can show and hide as needed. By default, the Standard and Formatting toolbars will appear automatically once the application, or an associated file, is opened.

A menu displays a list of commands. Some of the commands have images next to them so that you can quickly associate an image with an instruction. Most menus are located on the menu bar at the top of the application window. Some have sub-menus that enable access to further commands while others have keyboard shortcuts (executed by the simultaneous pressing of a combination of keys eg **Ctrl+P** = **Print** dialogue box) that, when committed to memory, help in the completion of a task quickly.

Additional pop-up menus are available when you right-click text, objects or other items.

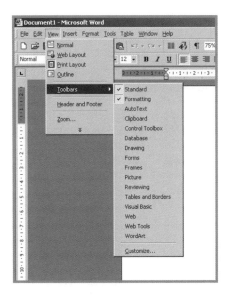

Open Microsoft Word.

From the menu bar, select **View** then **Toolbars**. The Standard and Formatting toolbars should already be selected (indicated by a tick).

Click the Drawing toolbar. This should now appear at the foot of your screen.

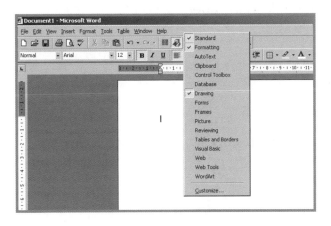

Move the pointer tool over any toolbar at the head or the foot of the screen. Right-click the mouse to once again activate the Toolbar menu. Click the **Drawing** option to remove the Drawing toolbar from the screen.

The Standard Toolbar

As mentioned previously, the **Standard** and **Formatting** toolbars will appear by default once a new document is opened in Word. Most of the commands you will need to use in the successful completion of a standard text document are included here.

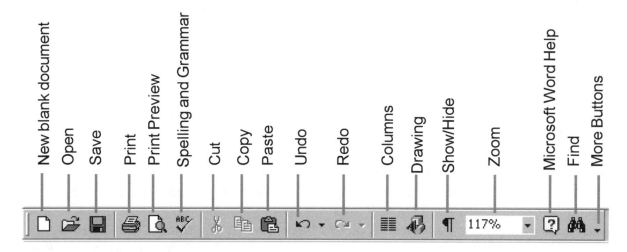

Keyboard Shortcuts

Selecting any of the drop-down boxes from the menu will display a number of commands with keyboard shortcuts (also known as 'quick keys').

For example, in order to print a document without using the **File** menu and **Print** option, press the **Control** and the letter **P** keys simultaneously (**Ctrl+P**).

Using the **Ctrl+P** quick keys option will activate the **Print** dialogue box from which a number of features can be employed.

Clicking the **Print** option from the Standard toolbar will send your document straight to the printer without the intervention of the dialogue box.

You can also press the **Alt** key and the underlined letter in the menu, ie **Alt+F** will open the **File** menu. Once opened, you can enter the respective letter to open another dialogue box. For example, once you have the **File** menu opened, you can press the letter **O** to open a new document.

T A S K		
	1.	**Open a blank document in Word.**
	2.	**Have a look at the different toolbars available.**
	3.	**Go through the menu items and try using different methods to open further dialogue boxes.**
	4.	**Leave your document open.**

The Mouse/Pointer Device

The movements of the on-screen pointer are mirrored by the movements of your mouse. Commands on the toolbars and the various options from each menu can be selected using the pointer tool. Items can be selected and text highlighted using the pointer tool.

The following are examples of the mouse pointer tools at various stages when using Word.

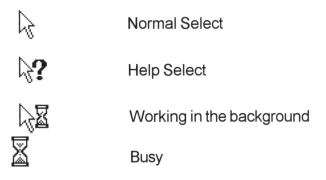

Normal Select

Help Select

Working in the background

Busy

Click And Type Pointer Shapes

As you then move the I-Beam pointer ⬚ over your Word document, the pointer shape indicates what text formatting will be applied to the document once you double-click the left mouse button.

From the **Tools** menu, click **Options** then the **Edit** tab and select the **Enable click and type** check box then click **OK**.

The following are examples of I-Beam pointer shapes.

Left align		Right align	
Centre		Left indent	
Left text wrap		Right text wrap	

T A S K	1. Using your open document, select Tools, Options and select the Enable click and type check box.
	2. Move your mouse over the screen to see if the I-Beam changes to show different alignments.

Navigating The Operating Environment

With most software applications there is often a number of ways to perform the same instructions using a variety of techniques. Using a combination of toolbars, menus, quick keys and your mouse pointer tool, all the features Windows has to offer can be employed in the creation of documents that have been quickly and efficiently authored.

Using The Scroll Bars

Most of the Office applications have scroll bars. These indicate that further information is available but cannot fit in the window. Clicking the **up/down** or **left/right** arrow will move the document so that more of the document can be viewed.

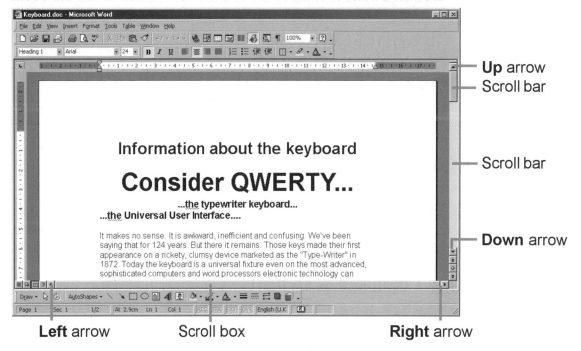

Use the **up/down** and **left/right** arrows to scroll up or down the page and left or right to move from side to side (this is only available if the page does not fit in the window).

Or click on the **Scroll Box**, keeping the mouse button pressed, drag up/down or left/right to move through the document.

Or point and click into the **Scroll Bar** with the mouse to go to a different place in the document.

Using The Keyboard

Basic keystrokes for moving around your document:

→	Moves the cursor across one character to the right
←	Moves the cursor across one character to the left
↓	Moves the cursor down one line
↑	Moves the cursor up one line
\<Page Down\>	Moves the cursor down one screen on each press
\<Page Up\>	Moves the cursor up one screen on each press
\<End\>	Moves the cursor to the end of the line
\<Home\>	Moves the cursor to the beginning of a line

The following combinations are used with the **Ctrl** key. When using a combination the **Ctrl** key must be pressed and held down whilst the other key is pressed. Release both together once action has been completed.

\<Ctrl\>\<Home\>	Moves to the beginning of the document
\<Ctrl\>\<End\>	Moves to the end of the document

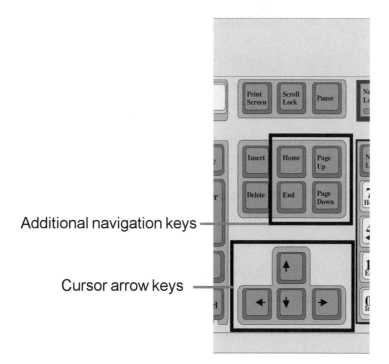

Additional navigation keys

Cursor arrow keys

Page Magnification And Zoom

The size of the document on screen can be customised by using the zoom facility. Zoom settings are in percentage format and range from 10% to 500%. Changing the zoom setting for a document will not affect a printed output, ie it does not increase or decrease text sizes etc - it controls how much of the document can be viewed on the screen.

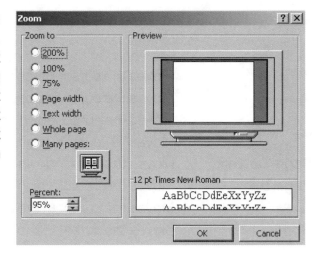

Select **View**, **Zoom** from the menu bar to display the **Zoom** dialogue box.

The **Zoom to** section allows you to change the settings by clicking on a radio button (round button).

The **Many pages, Whole page** and **Text width** options are only available if you are viewing the document in **Print Layout** view. Viewing many pages will allow you to view up to 42 pages at a time by clicking on the **Monitor** button.

A custom zoom setting can be entered in the **Percent** box.

The **Preview** pane on the right of the dialogue box will display how the zoom setting will look together with a preview of the font and font size. Click **OK** to apply the settings or **Cancel** to abandon.

Another method of changing the zoom setting is to use the **Zoom** drop-down list on the Standard toolbar.

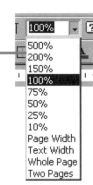

Click on the drop-down arrow to display the options available. **Whole pages** and **Two pages** are only available if you are viewing your document in print layout view.

You can either select one of the % zoom values shown by clicking it or type in a new setting, then press enter to apply it.

T A S K	1.	Practise changing the zoom settings to 200%, 50% and Whole Page.
	2.	Finish on a zoom setting which is suitable for you to work on.

Print Preview A Document

The purpose of print preview is to display the document as it will look when printed. By using this feature before you print, the document can be checked for layout, orientation and margins etc. Viewing a page before printing saves wasted print, ie paper and ink. Print preview is known as a **WYSIWYG** feature (**W**hat **Y**ou **S**ee **I**s **W**hat **Y**ou **G**et) - the document that you see on screen will match the printed document.

Print preview will open in its own window and has its own toolbar. To return back to your document click on the **Close** button.

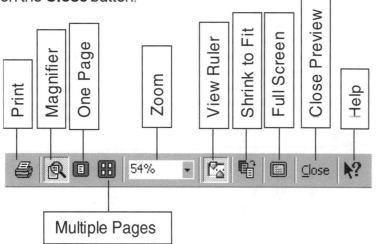

Multiple Pages

The Print Preview Window

Notice that the document name will still appear on the title bar, but the word 'Preview' will also appear in brackets to indicate that you are previewing the document. The document will appear as it will be printed on paper.

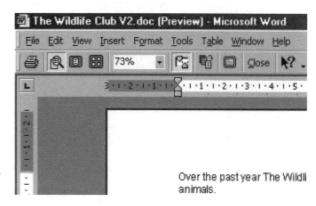

Error Messages And Prompts

Error messages and prompt dialogue boxes appear on-screen if you've forgotten to perform a particular task or function, such as the following error message:

Simply follow the instructions given on the dialogue box and choose from the available options.

T A S K	1.	Close the word processing application. Click No to saving the changes when prompted.

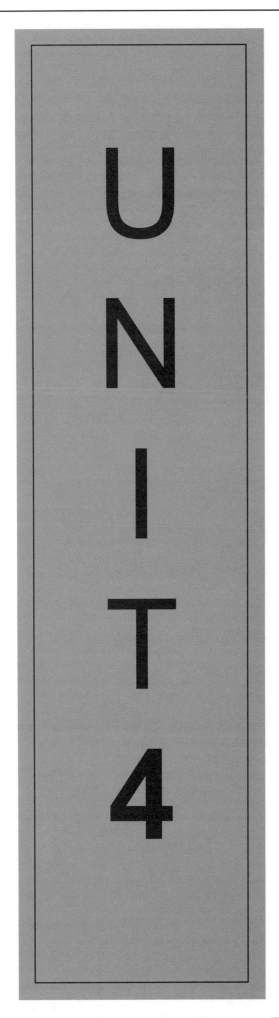

On completion of this unit you will have learnt about and practised the following:

File Management Systems
- Open Windows Explorer
- Windows Explorer Screen
- Explorer Toolbar
- Files And Folders (Directories)

Explorer Hierarchy
- Hierarchy Displayed In Diagram Form

File Types
- Types Of File
- Office Filename Extensions
- How To Change The Views
- Changing The Appearance Of The List Of Folders And Files

Sorting Files
- File Type View
- Sorting Within Details View

File Management Systems

Windows 2000 can be used to organise your work into a hierarchy of files and folders that will enable you to locate and store files quickly.

Imagine trying to find the January to March 1999 gas bill if all bills are kept in the corner of your sitting room or working in an office that kept all of its correspondence in a large cardboard box. The files you create and save to your floppy disk can be organised like files in a filing cabinet.

Windows 2000 provides two ways of managing files and folders:

1. **Windows Explorer**   Useful for viewing the hierarchical or branching structure of the disc and its folders. Folders are opened up to reveal the sub-folders and files within.

2. **My Computer**   Useful for viewing the contents of a single folder or drive. The contents of the item selected are displayed in a new window.

Open Windows Explorer

Click **Start**
    Programs
    Accessories
    Windows Explorer.

Title bar   **Menu bar**   **Toolbar**   **Address bar**

Left Pane   **Scroll bar**   **Right Pane**   **Scroll bar**

Windows Explorer Screen

If you prefer to look at your files in a hierarchical structure, you'll like using Windows Explorer. Instead of opening drives and folders in separate windows, you can browse through them in a single window. The left side of the Windows Explorer window contains a list of your drives and folders, and the right side displays the content of a selected folder. You can use the **View** menu to change how the files in the right pane will appear, your screen may appear different to that shown previously.

Title bar   Displays the Explorer icon and the folder or drive that is being explored.

Menu bar   Contains the main Explorer menus, where a selection of commands are available.

Toolbar   Displays buttons that you can select using the mouse to perform commonly needed tasks. If the toolbar is not showing click **View**, **Toolbars**, **Standard Buttons**.

Address bar   Displays the location of a selected file. If the toolbar is not showing click **View**, **Toolbars**, **Address Bar**.

Scroll bars   Used to navigate around the panes to view all information.

Left pane   Is the Explorer bar which displays the drives and folders available.

Right pane   Displays the contents of the drive or folder selected in the left pane.

Explorer Toolbar

As with the applications you have been using before, Explorer has a toolbar with icons giving shortcuts to the following tasks. Reading from left to right they are:

- **Back** moves the view through previously selected folders or drives.

- **Forward** moves the view forward through the previously selected series of folders and files.

- Go **Up** one folder in the hierarchy.

- **Search** for files and folders anywhere on the computer.

- **Folders** creates a new window pane from which you can access all the drives on your computer.

- **History** provide links to all the web sites that have been visited on the Internet during the last three weeks.

- **Move to** allows you to cut and paste a document from one location to another.

- **Copy to** allows you to copy and paste a document from one location to another.

- **Delete** a file or folder or multiple files or folders.

- **Undo** the last action.

- Change the **Views** of the files and folders in the right pane.

Files And Folders (Directories)

Directory is another word for folder.

The files you create and save to your floppy disk can be organised like files in an office, placed into folders that are placed in drawers in a filing cabinet. The term 'file' in this context, refers to a single piece of work such as a letter or report, a spreadsheet, a drawing or a set of records from a database.

In the same way that loose papers in the traditional office are organised into folders, computer files are grouped into electronic folders. This makes it easier to find a particular piece of work. File management tasks such as copying or deleting groups of files are much simpler.

Folders are displayed with the following icon:

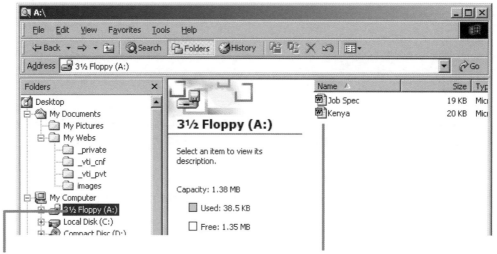

Select the drive or folder by clicking on it once.

This results in the folders and files (contents of the drive or folder selected) being displayed in the right pane.

> **T A S K**
>
> 1.   **Select the 3½ Floppy (A:) (floppy disk drive) to view its contents.**

Click on the **-** signs to compact the drives or folders to hide folders or sub- folders within.

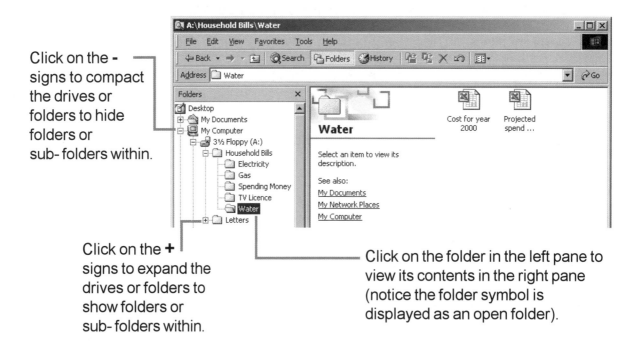

Click on the **+** signs to expand the drives or folders to show folders or sub- folders within.

Click on the folder in the left pane to view its contents in the right pane (notice the folder symbol is displayed as an open folder).

A **sub-folder** is a folder within another folder. The screen above shows the **Household Bills** folder containing the following sub-folders: **Electricity**, **Gas**, **Spending Money**, **TV Licence** and **Water**.

> **T A S K**
>
> 1.   **Find and view the contents of the Water folder located on your floppy disk.**

Explorer Hierarchy

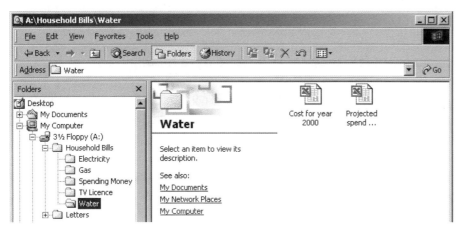

Drive	3½ Floppy (A:)
Folder	Household Bills
Sub folder	Water
Files	Cost for year 2000.xls
	Projected spend for 2001.xls

NB Only contents of one folder or sub-folder can be viewed at a time. To view the contents of another folder, ie Gas, the Gas folder must be selected.

Hierarchy Displayed In Diagram Form

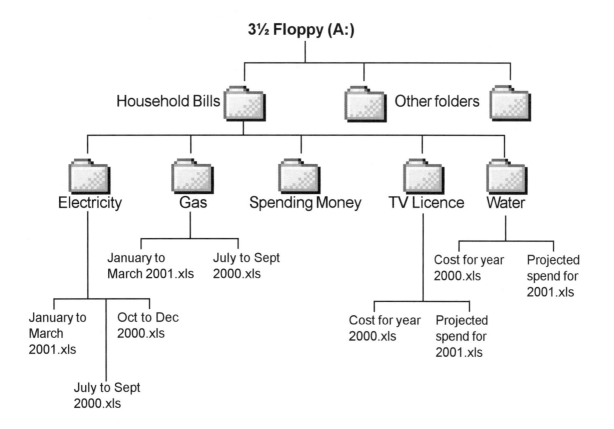

File Types

Types Of File

There are two main categories of file; **program files** and **data files**.

Program files make up the software applications such as Microsoft Office and Windows 2000 itself. You should not attempt to modify or move these files. Program files have extensions like **.exe**.

Data files cover everything you produce, ranging from word processing text, database and spreadsheet files to pictures and music. They are often referred to as **documents**.

The most widely used **types of data file** are created by saving in one of the applications, such as Word. When this is done, an icon is attached to the file name to indicate the type of file eg:

Word   Access

Excel   Paint

HTML web document   PageMaker publication

JPEG document   Adobe Acrobat document

Most of the files will be either text, graphic, audio or video files. Some may be compressed, others not. The most common compressed files are those with extensions like **.ZIP**, **.SIT** and **.TAR**. These extensions represent popular compression formats for the PC, Macintosh and UNIX. They may be single files or groups of files that have been bundled together into a single **archive**. An archive file can contain video or graphics files, and often contains software programs with related documentation. Occasionally you may encounter files with multiple extensions like .tar.gz, which usually means more than one type of software was used to compile and compress the file.

The following are some popular examples of file types and their headings

Plain text files

.html/.htm The language in which web documents are authored requires a web browser, such as Navigator or Internet Explorer, for viewing.

.txt The simplest and most common text file type.

Formatted Documents

.doc A common PC format for formatted text files. File type: ASCII.

.pdf Portable Document Format, a proprietary format developed by Adobe Systems, Inc. that allows formatted documents to be transferred over the Internet so they look the same on any computer.

This file type requires the Adobe Acrobat Reader to view files and can be downloaded from the Adobe web site.

.ps A PostScript file. Though it is technically a plain text file, it is essentially unreadable except by a PostScript printer or with the help of an on-screen viewer like Ghostscript, which is available for Mac, Windows and UNIX.

Compressed and Encoded Files

.bin A Mac Binary II Encoded File. This file type requires Stuffit Expander for the Mac. You download this type of file as MacBinary or Binary.

.exe A DOS or Windows program or a self-extracting file. If this is an executable (self-extracting) file, then it can usually be launched by double-clicking on the icon on your Desktop. This is the only way to tell if it is an executable file.

.sea A Macintosh self-extracting archive file. An archive file is usually a collection of files that have been combined into one to make it easy to download. Because the archive is self-extracting, you don't need any special application or utility to launch it. You simply click on the icon from the Macintosh desktop and it decompresses and unbundles the files.

.tar/.tar.gz/.tar.Z/.tgz A Unix archiving scheme that is also available for PCs. Tar, which is short for Tape ARchive, can archive files but not compress them, so .tar files are often gzipped, which is why you might occasionally encounter the file extension .tar.gz. To download and use .tar files on a Mac, you use a program called Tar. For Windows you can use WinZip to view and extract archive files.

.zip A common compression standard for DOS and Windows that uses a DOS utility called PKZIP. These files can be decompressed on the PC with WinZIP. You can get copies for Windows 3.1 and Windows 95/98/2000 (winzipXX.exe). You can also use Stuffit Expander for Mac or Windows.

Graphics files

.gif The most common graphics file format on the Internet, it stands for Graphics Interchange Format. If your browser does not have a built-in GIF viewer, then you can use Lview Pro (lviewpxx.zip) or PolyView (polyvxxx.zip) to view these graphics on a Windows PC. On the Mac, a shareware utility called GIF Converter can be used to view and modify GIFs.

.jpg/.jpeg/.jfif A popular compression standard used for photos and still images. JPEG files can be viewed on any platform as long as you have a JPEG viewer. You can view JPEG files with most web browsers. For the Mac, use JPEGView; for the PC, you can use Lview Pro or PolyView.

.tiff A very large, high-resolution image format. Use JPEGView for the Mac and Lview Pro or PolyView for the PC.

Sound Files

.mp3 is the most popular file format on the Web for distributing CD-quality music. A 1Mb file is equal to about one minute of music. This type of file requires an MP3 player, which is available for both Macintosh and Windows.

.wav The native sound format for Windows. On the Mac, you can use Sound App to play .wav files. For the PC, use Waveform Hold and Modify or Goldwave to play these files. There is also a good program called Win Play that will play it, as well as other popular formats.

Video Files

.avi The standard video format for Windows. These files need an AVI Video for Windows player (aviprox.exe) or the Windows Media Player from Microsoft.

.mov/.movie The common format for QuickTime movies, the Macintosh native movie platform. QuickTime is also available for Windows.

.mpg/mpeg A standard format for 'movies' on the Internet, using the MPEG compression scheme. There are a variety of MPEG Players for Windows and an MPEG FTP site that has a large collection of MPEG player resources for all platforms (Mac, Windows and Unix).

T A S K		
	1.	**Can you name the two main categories of files?**
	2.	**Name two of the most common compression file extensions.**
	3.	**What piece of software is required in order for you to view a .htm web document?**
	4.	**Zip/exe and tar files come under the heading of what file type?**
	5.	**Open Microsoft Explorer and view the hierarchical content of the A: drive. Produce screen print and a printout.**
	6.	**Close Microsoft Explorer.**

Office Filename Extensions

When a file is created by saving in one of the applications, such as Excel, a four character extension is applied alongside the filename. On opening a file the four character extension tells the computer which application to open to access the file contents.

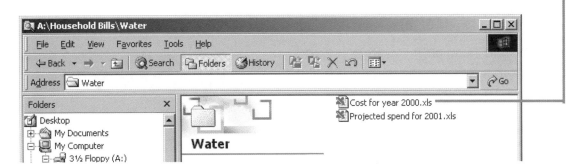

If the file extensions are hidden, click **Tools**, **Folder Options** and the **View** tab.

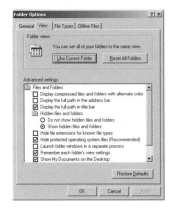

To display the file extensions, remove the tick in the box to the left of:
Hide file extensions for known file types

Click **OK** to accept change.

NB   File extensions are usually visible, but this is not always the case. File extensions can be hidden from view by following the above method, but can be replacing a tick to the left of Hide file extensions for known file types.

Data file extensions common to Microsoft Office

Microsoft Word	**.doc**
Text only document	**.txt**
Rich Text Format	**.rtf**
Microsoft Excel	**.xls**
Microsoft Access	**.mdb**
Microsoft PowerPoint	**.ppt** or **.pps**
Microsoft Paint	**.bmp**

Filename extensions consist of a full stop followed by three letters making up the four character extension.

T A S K		
	1.	**View the floppy disk content and the types of file it contains.**
	2.	**List the file type heading(s) under which each file type appears.**

How To Change The Views

The appearance of Explorer can be altered and manipulated to suit your favourite style - the concept of organising files does not change.

Working in Web Style

Work in Web style if you prefer to organise and browse your computer contents using Web-like options.

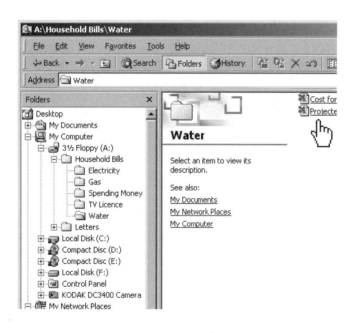

Click **Tools**.
Click **Folder Options**.
From **Web View** select.
Enable Web content in folders.

Select
- **Single-click to open an item (point to select)**
- **Underline icon titles consistent with my browser.**

Click **OK**.

To select an item, move the mouse pointer over the file or folder you wish to select. The pointer will change to a pointing hand. The name of the selected item is displayed on a blue background.

To open a file from Windows Explorer, click once.

Working in Classic Style

Click **Tools**.
Click **Folder Options**.
General tab.
Click **Use Windows classic folders**.

Click **OK**.

To select items, move the mouse
pointer over the file or folder you
wish to select, then click the left
mouse button once.

When selected, the item shows
with a dark blue background.

To open a file from Windows
Explorer, click to select the file
and press the **Enter** key.

| T A S K | 1. | Change the Windows Explorer appearance to Web style. Practise selecting files and opening folders. Close any files accidentally opened by clicking on the cross or Close button in the top right-hand corner of the opened application. |
| | 2. | Change the Windows Explorer appearance to Classic style. Practise selecting files and opening folders. Again, close any files accidentally opened by clicking on the cross or Close button in the top right-hand corner of the opened application. |

Changing The Appearance Of The List Of Folders And Files

Click on the drop-down arrow next to **Views**.

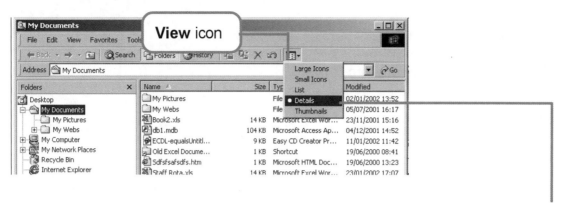

This displays choices available - the option already selected is indicated with a bullet.

Alternatively, click the **View** icon - this changes the view by running through the list of options one by one.

The files and folders are not affected in any other way except the appearance of the list in the right hand pane. An example of each is illustrated below:

Large Icons

Small Icons

List

Details

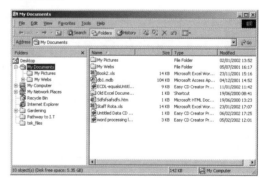

Thumbnails

NB   Details - displays file size, type and date last modified.

T A S K	**1.** Practise switching between views. **2.** Select Details view before moving on.

Sorting Files

File Type View

Finding files can be made easier by sorting the files by name, size, type or date modified. These features represent the properties and attributes of the file.

Click **View**.

Click **Arrange Icons**.

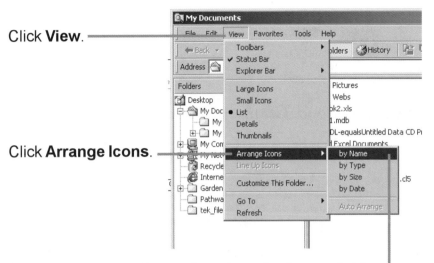

Choose the type of file-sort from the selection available.

Sorting Within Details View

Click on the column titles to sort the contents.

Name	Size	Type	Modified
My Webs		File Folder	05/07/2001 16:17
My Pictures		File Folder	02/01/2002 13:52
Old Excel Docume...	1 KB	Shortcut	19/06/2000 08:41
Sdfsfsafsdfs.htm	1 KB	Microsoft HTML Doc...	19/06/2000 13:23
Book2.xls	14 KB	Microsoft Excel Wor...	23/11/2001 15:16

T A S K

1. **Practise sorting the contents by name, type, size and date modified.
    Sort by name order before continuing.**

C O N S O L I D A T I O N E X E R C I S E	1. Using Microsoft Explorer, access and select the 3½ Floppy (A:) (floppy disk drive) to view the files it contains. 2. Find and view and name the contents of the Household Bills folder located on your floppy disk. 3. Can you name two files extensions belonging to the Sound file format? 4. mpeg/mov and avi. come under which file-type heading? 5. Name the file type extension that has to be viewed through Windows Explorer. 6. Jpeg/gif and tiff files come under what heading of file type? 7. View the hierarchical content of the A: drive as seen through Explorer. Produce a screenshot of the Explorer window, paste it into a Word document and produce a printout. Close Microsoft Explorer. 8. View the floppy disk content and name the types of file extension(s) it contains. 9. List the file type heading(s) under which each file type appears. 10. Once again, change the Windows Explorer appearance to Web style, then practise selecting files and opening folders. Close any files accidentally opened by clicking on the cross or Close button in the top right-hand corner of the opened application. 11. Once more, change the Windows Explorer appearance to Classic style, then practise selecting files and opening folders. Again, close any files accidentally opened by clicking on the cross or Close button in the top right-hand corner of the opened application. 12. Practise sorting the contents by name, type, size and date modified. Sort by name order before continuing.

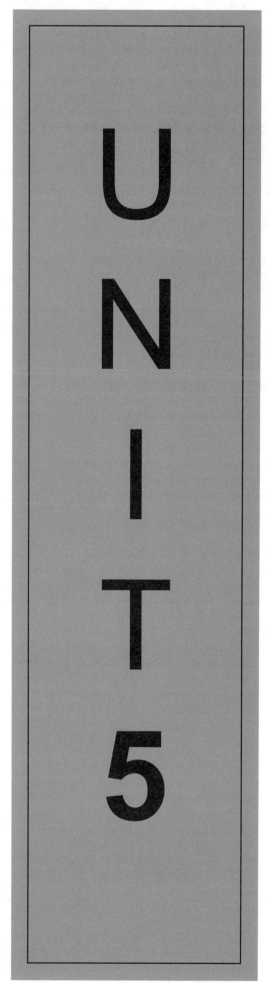

On completion of this unit you will have learnt about and practised the following:

Creating Folders (Directories) In Windows Explorer

- Creating Folders (Directories)
- Creating Sub-folders (Sub-directories)
- Moving Files
- Copying Files
- Multiple File Selection

Renaming Files And Folders

- Renaming Files
- Renaming Folders
- Deleting Files Or Folders
- Using The Recycle Bin
- Backup A File or Folder Onto A Floppy Disk
- Creating A Backup File On The Same Floppy Disk
- Creating A Backup File rom The Hard Disk Onto A Floppy Disk

Creating Folders (Directories) In Windows Explorer

Creating Folders (Directories)

'Directory' is another word for 'folder'. Folders can contain many files and sub-folders, they should be given names that you will be able to recognise instantly, rather than having to open each folder and view the contents.

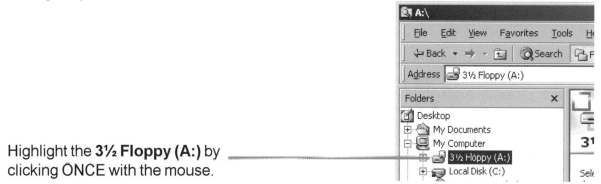

Highlight the **3½ Floppy (A:)** by clicking ONCE with the mouse.

Select **File**, **New**, **Folder**.

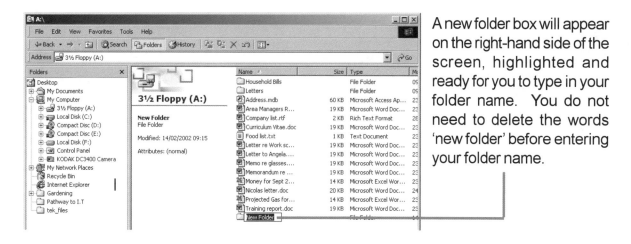

A new folder box will appear on the right-hand side of the screen, highlighted and ready for you to type in your folder name. You do not need to delete the words 'new folder' before entering your folder name.

Type in the folder name and press **Enter**.

If the new folder cannot be seen on the left-hand side of the screen, click on the **+** next to the **3½ Floppy (A:)** and the folder with the name you typed in will appear.

You have now created a folder that you can move or copy files into.

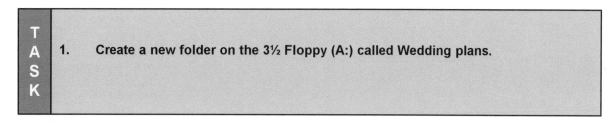

TASK

1.　Create a new folder on the 3½ Floppy (A:) called Wedding plans.

Creating Sub-folders (Sub-directories)

A sub-folder is a folder within another folder.

The **Address bar** displays what has been selected.
In this example: **A:\Wedding plans**
the Wedding plans folder on the floppy disk drive (A:).

Highlight the folder in which you want to create the new folder.

Select **File**, **New**, **Folder**.

The new folder box will appear on the right hand side of the screen, highlighted and ready for you to type in your folder name.

Type in the folder name and press **Enter**.

On the left hand side of the screen, click on the **+** next to the folder. This will show the new sub-folder you have created.

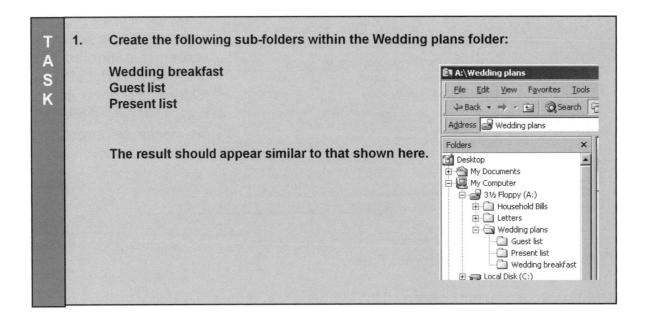

T A S K	1.	Create the following sub-folders within the Wedding plans folder:
		Wedding breakfast **Guest list** **Present list**
		The result should appear similar to that shown here.

Moving Files

After files have been saved you may wish to move them from one location to another.

Select the file you wish to move (cut).

> Click **Edit**.
> Click **Cut**.

or

Click on the **Cut** button on the toolbar.

Click on the folder or drive to where you wish to move the file (left pane). Check the address bar to ensure that the correct location has been selected.

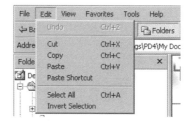

> Click **Edit**.
> Click **Paste**.

or

Click on the **Paste Shortcut** option.

This will move a file from its original location to its new location.

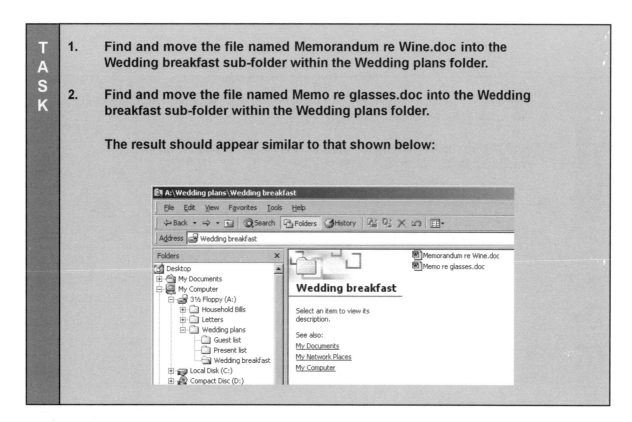

T A S K	1.	Find and move the file named Memorandum re Wine.doc into the Wedding breakfast sub-folder within the Wedding plans folder.
	2.	Find and move the file named Memo re glasses.doc into the Wedding breakfast sub-folder within the Wedding plans folder.

The result should appear similar to that shown below:

Copying Files

You may wish to copy a file and place a copy of the file into another location. Copying enables duplicate copies of files to be made.

Select the file you wish to copy.

> Click **Edit**.
> Click **Copy**.

or

Click on the **Copy To** button on the toolbar.

Click on the folder or the drive where you wish to place the duplicate file (left pane). Check the address bar to ensure that the correct location has been selected.

> Click **Edit**.
> Click **Paste**.

or

Click on the **Paste Shortcut** option.

This will make a copy of the file in the selected location.

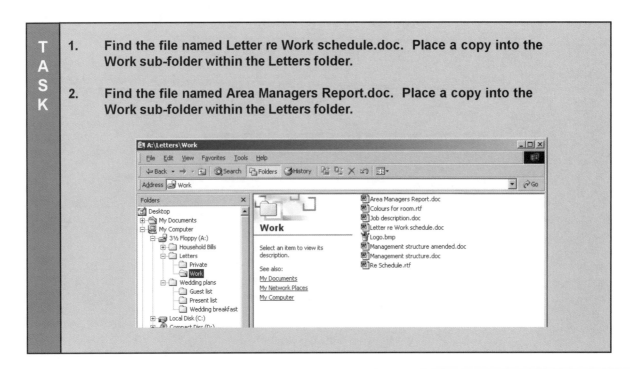

> T
> A
> S
> K
>
> 1. Find the file named **Letter re Work schedule.doc**. Place a copy into the **Work** sub-folder within the **Letters** folder.
>
> 2. Find the file named **Area Managers Report.doc**. Place a copy into the **Work** sub-folder within the **Letters** folder.

Multiple File Selection

Multiple file selection increases efficiency, allowing the user to move or copy more than one file at a time.

Selecting a group of files together

Select the first file in the group.

Press and hold the **Shift** key (above the **Ctrl** key) in the lower left-hand corner on the keyboard.

Select the last file in the group
(all the file names in the group will be highlighted).

Release the **Shift** key.

Commands made will apply to all the highlighted files.

NB Highlighting mistakes can be de-selected by clicking anywhere in a blank area.

Selecting multiple files that are not grouped together

Click on one of the files that
you wish to select.

Press and hold the control (**Ctrl**) key on the keyboard.

Click on each of the files you wish to
select, one at a time.

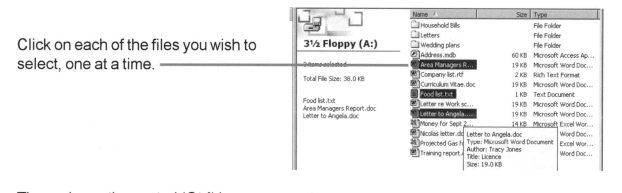

Then release the control (**Ctrl**) key.

Any commands that are now made, ie copy or cut, will apply to the highlighted files.

**NB   Highlighting mistakes can be de-selected one at a time. Press the Ctrl key,
then click on a highlighted file to de-select it.**

T A S K	**1.**	**Practise selecting and de-selecting multiple files.**
	2.	**Then practise selecting files that are not grouped.**

Renaming Files And Folders

Files and folders can be renamed to reflect their content more accurately or to correct any entry errors.

Renaming files

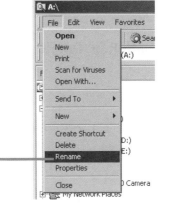

Highlight the file you wish to rename.

Click **File**, **Rename**

The file name will be highlighted. Place the cursor over the selected file name Place the **I-Beam** before the file extension.

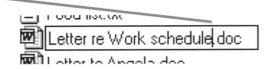

Backspace the filename and type in the new name. **You must ensure that the full file extension (including full stop) is left in place.**

Press the **Enter** key to accept the change.

T A S K	1.	**Change the filename of the document called 'Letter re Work schedule.doc' to 'Work Schedule 20-09-01.doc'**

Renaming Folders

Highlight the folder you wish to rename.

Click **File**, **Rename**

The folder is highlighted, enabling you to type in the new folder name. Folders do not require an extension.

Press the **Enter** key to accept the change.

T A S K	1.	**Change the Letters folder to Communication**

Deleting Files Or Folders

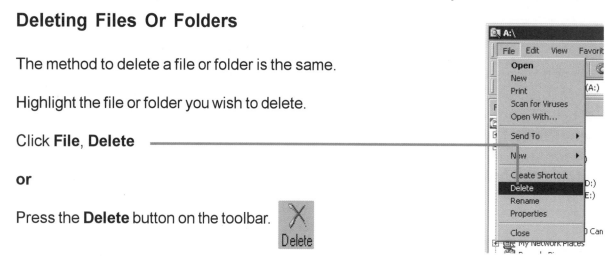

The method to delete a file or folder is the same.

Highlight the file or folder you wish to delete.

Click **File**, **Delete** —————————————————

or

Press the **Delete** button on the toolbar.

A confirm file or folder delete dialogue box will appear. Click **Yes** to confirm deletion.

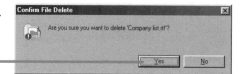

If deleting a folder, all of its contents will be deleted including sub-folders and files. —————————

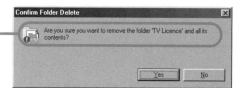

T A S K		
	1.	Delete the file called Company list.rtf.
	2.	Delete the folder called TV Licence and all its contents.
	3.	Close Windows Explorer.

Using The Recycle Bin

Files deleted from a floppy disk are not recoverable, but files deleted from the hard drive are placed into a folder called the **Recycle Bin.** These files will remain in the Recycle Bin until you decide to empty it. These files can be restored to their original locations.

Double-click the **Recycle Bin** icon on the Desktop.

To Restore a file

Click on the file you wish to restore.
Click **File**.
Click **Restore**.
The file will be restored to its
original location.

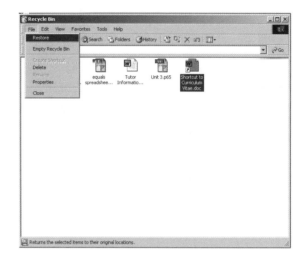

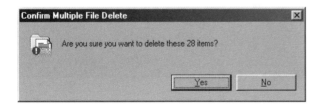

To Empty the Recycle Bin

Click **File**.
Click **Empty Recycle Bin**.
Click **Yes** to empty the bin.

NB The Recycle Bin should be emptied regularly to free up disk space.

NB Files and folders deleted from a floppy disk are not retrievable, but files and folders deleted from the hard drive (C:) are placed in a folder called the Recycle Bin from which they can be retrieved.

T A S K		
	1.	**Copy the Curriculum Vitae file into My Documents on the C: drive.**
	2.	**Delete the file.**
	3.	**Restore the file.**
	4.	**Delete the file and empty Recycle Bin.**

CONSOLIDATION TASK

1. Change the Communications folder back to Letters.

2. Create a folder with the name Meeting on the A: drive.

3. Create a document with the filename Corporate Agenda.doc.
   Move the newly created file into the folder called Meeting.

4. Create a new folder with the name Office Administration.

5. Place the folder Meeting in the folder Office Administration so that it now becomes a sub-folder.

6. Practise selecting and de-selecting multiple files.

7. Practise selecting files that are not grouped.

8. Rename the file Corporate Agenda.doc into Corporate ID.doc.

9. Find the file named Area Managers Report.doc. Place a copy into the Meeting sub-folder within the Office Administration folder.

10. Find and move the files named Company list.rtf and TV Licence into the sub-folder Meeting contained in the folder Office Administration situated on the A: drive.

11. View the folder Office Administration within Microsoft Explorer.

12. Delete the folder Office Administration and all its contents.

13. Close Windows Explorer.

Backup A File or Folder Onto A Floppy Disk

The internal hard disk is generally a well-designed component that can perform reliably for many thousands of hours over several years. However, it is by no means uncommon for individuals and even companies to 'lose' the entire contents of a hard disk due to accidents and natural disasters. The only way to reduce the risk of a computing catastrophe is to make duplicate or backup copies of all important files. Ideally the backup copy should be on a removable disk (floppy, zip or CD) that will allow it to be stored in a safe place.

Creating A Backup File On The Same Floppy Disk

Using Windows Explorer or My Computer, create a folder on the floppy disk called **Backup**.

Select the file. Copy the file you wish to backup and place the copy in the backup folder. Rename the file so that the name indicates it is a backup.

T A S K	1.	Create a folder called Backup on the 3½ Floppy (A:).
	2.	Copy the file called Curriculum Vitae.doc to the Backup folder.
	3.	Rename the file so that it reads Curriculum Vitae backup.doc.

Creating A Backup File From The Hard Disk Onto A Floppy Disk

Using Windows Explorer or My Computer, locate the file or folder on the hard drive that you wish to backup to floppy disk.

Select the file or folder click **Edit** then **Copy**. Paste the copy onto the floppy disk.

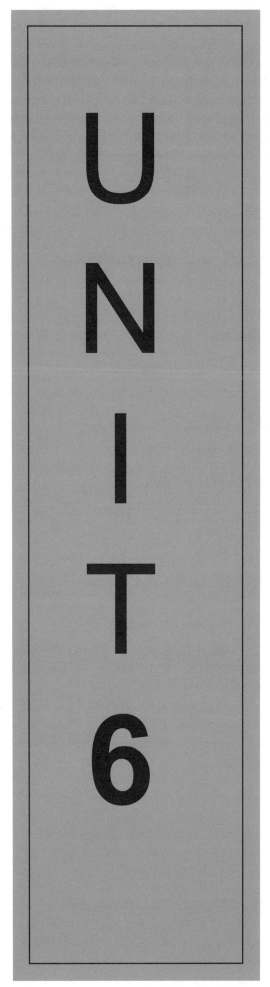

On completion of this unit you will have learnt about and practised the following:

File Management Within My Computer
- My Computer Screen
- My Computer Menu Bar
- Creating Sub-folders (Sub-directories)
- Moving Files
- Copying Files
- Copying Files By Dragging And Dropping
- Move Files By Dragging And Dropping
- Renaming Files And Folders
- Deleting Files And Folders

Finding Files
- Finding A File
- Finding The File By Name
- Finding The File By Date
- Finding the File By The File Type

Viewing Printer Settings
- Printing From An Installed Printer
- Viewing A Print Job's Progress
- How To Change The Default Printer

File Management Within My Computer

Double-click the **My Computer** icon on the Desktop.

or

Hover the mouse over the **My Computer** icon.

Click the right mouse button.

Click **Open** from the menu.

My Computer Screen

My Computer is useful for viewing the contents of a single folder or drive. Their contents are displayed in a new window. My Computer gives an immediate view of the different disk storage devices, the Control Panel and Printers. The My Computer window may need to be resized so that all the icons are visible.

My Computer Menu Bar

From the My Computer menu bar there are a number of familiar (and some not so familiar) options with which to alter the display of the information in your window.

Creating Sub-folders (Sub-directories)

Double-click the folder in which you wish to create the sub-folder.

Look at the **Address** bar to ensure the correct folder or drive has been selected.

Click **File**
   New
   Folder.

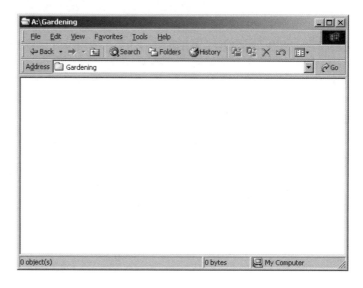

A new folder box will appear in the window, highlighted and ready to overtype the new folder name.

Type in the folder name
and press the **Enter** key.

T A S K	1.	Create the following sub-folders within the Gardening folder:

Patio
Flowers
Costs

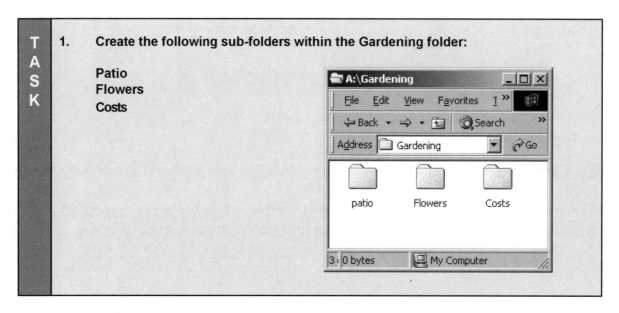

Moving Files

Select the file you wish to move (cut).

      Click **Edit**.
      Click **Cut**.

or

Click on the **Cut** button on the toolbar.

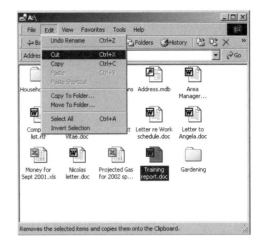

Double-click to open the folder containing the sub-folder you would like to move the file into.

Then double-click to open the sub-folder where you want to move the file to.

      Click **Edit**.
      Click **Paste**.

or

Click on the **Paste Shortcut** option.

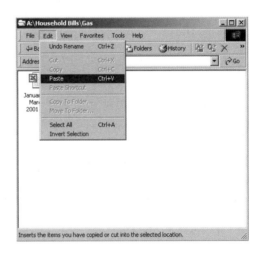

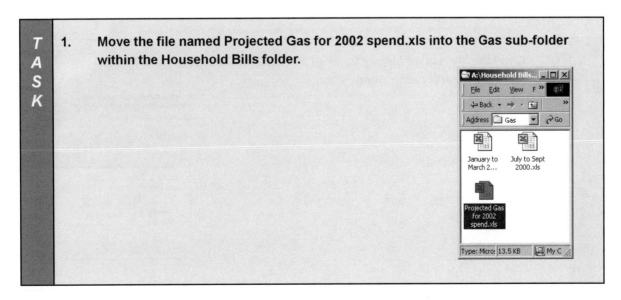

TASK

1.   **Move the file named Projected Gas for 2002 spend.xls into the Gas sub-folder within the Household Bills folder.**

Copying Files

Select the file that you would like
to copy (duplicate).

      Click **Edit**.
      Click **Copy**.

or

Click on the **Copy To**
button on the toolbar.

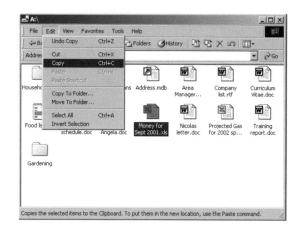

Double-click to open the folder containing the sub-folder you would like to copy the file to.
Then double-click to open the sub-folder you want to copy the file into.

      Click **Edit**.
      Click **Paste**.

or

Click on the **Paste Shortcut** option.

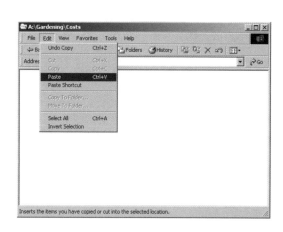

T A S K	1.	Copy the file named Money for Sept 2001.xls into the Costs sub-folder within the Gardening folder.

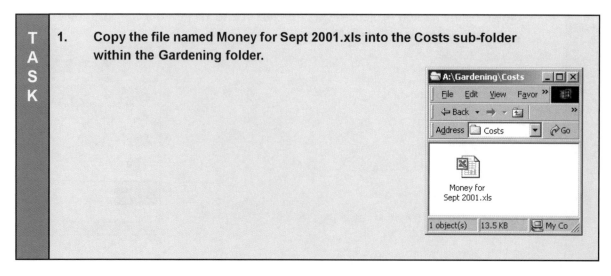

Copying Files By Dragging And Dropping

Open the **3½ Floppy (A:)**.

Identify the folder or sub-folder where you wish to place the file.

1. Select the file, keeping the left mouse button pressed.
2. Press the **Ctrl** key.
3. Drag to the new location.
4. Release the mouse button - a copy of the file will appear highlighted in its new location.
5. Release the **Ctrl** key.

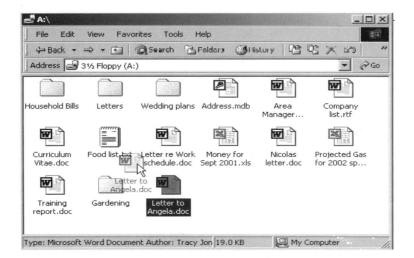

T A S K	1.	**Copy the file called Letter to Angela.doc to the Letters folder on your (A:) drive.**

Moving Files By Dragging And Dropping

Moving files by dragging and dropping is similar to copying, with one difference: the **Ctrl** key is not used.

Open the **3½ Floppy (A:)**.
Open the folder or sub-folder where you wish to place the file.
Select the file keeping the left mouse button pressed.
Drag to the new location.
Release the mouse button and the file will move to its new location.

T A S K	1.	Move the file called Nicolas letter.doc to the Letters folder on your (A:) drive.

Renaming Files And Folders

The method of renaming files and folders is exactly the same as the method shown for use in Windows Explorer.

Deleting Files And Folders

The method of deleting files and folders is exactly the same as the method shown for use in Windows Explorer.

T A S K	1.	Close all open windows including My Computer.

Finding Files

Finding A File

Finding files on a floppy disk or hard drive can take some time if files are not kept in an organised structure. The computer has a search facility to assist.

Click **Start**.

Click **Search**.

Click **Files or Folders**.

Finding The File By Name

Click on the **Name & Location** tab.

Type file names into the **Search for files or folders named:** text field.

Keywords within a document can be entered in this text field.

Ensure the **Look in:** box shows the **3½ Floppy (A:)**.

Click **Search Now**.

Files found that match the named criteria are displayed here.

The exact location of the file is shown here.

Double-click the file to open it.

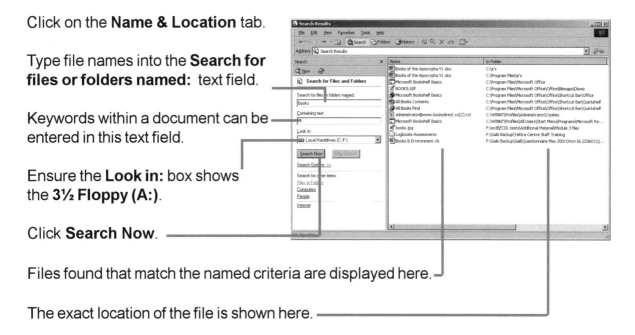

T A S K	1.	**Using the original floppy disk, find all files that have July in the title.**

Finding The File By Date

Ensure the **Look in:** box shows the **3½ Floppy (A:)** drive.

Click the **Search Options** link to find files by **Date**, **Type**, **Size** and **Advanced Options**.

Click the **Date** check box.

Select **files Modified**.

Select **between**.

The dates can be changed by clicking the drop-down arrow.

Select the month by clicking the backwards and forwards arrows and then select the date.

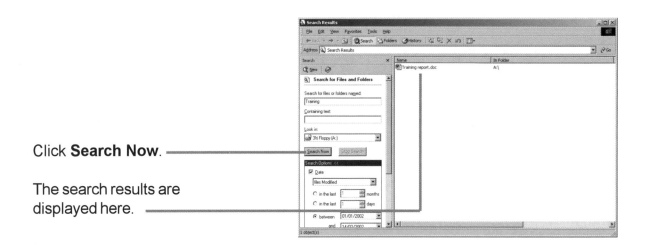

Click **Search Now**. ─────────────

The search results are displayed here. ─────────────

T A S K	1.	Find the files that have been modified between 20/02/02 and 22/02/02.

Finding The File By The File Type

Ensure the **Look in:** box shows the **3½ Floppy (A:)** drive.

Click in the **Type** check box.

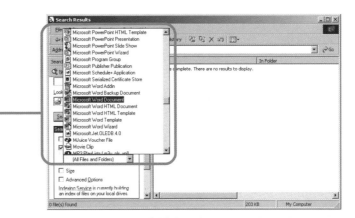

Click on the downward arrow in
the **All Files and Folders**
section. Select the required file
type from the available menu.

Click **Search Now**.

T A S K	1.	Find the files that were created with the word processing application.
	2.	Close the Search Results dialogue box.

Viewing Printer Settings

Printing From An Installed Printer

To print a document in the Windows operating environment:

Click **File**
    Print
    OK.

or

Click on the **Print** button on the toolbar.

T A S K	1.	**Print the Word document that you have open on your screen.**

Viewing A Print Job's Progress

The computer sends the data to the printer and sometimes this process can take longer than you expect. Many other people may be printing to the same printer, or a large file may be in the process of being printed. Don't add to the frustration by sending multiple copies of the same document.

If the printer receives two or more print jobs at one time, it holds them in the order that they were received. When a print job reaches the top of the line, the Spool manager sends the job to the printer.

The print icon will be displayed on the right-hand side of the taskbar.

To activate the Spool manager dialogue box as pictured below, double-click the print icon on the taskbar.

From the Spool manager, you can view print status information about the print jobs that have been sent to your printer. You can also cancel, pause and resume print jobs by right-clicking the mouse button within the dialogue box and selecting the appropriate option.

How To Change The Default Printer

Your computer may be on a network that may have more than one choice of printer installed. To change the default printer:

Click **File**.
Click **Print**.

Click on the drop-down arrow
next to the **Printer Name**.

Select the printer that you
wish to send the document to.

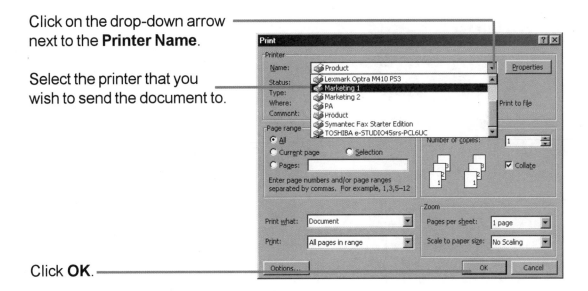

Click **OK**.

<table>
<tr><td rowspan="2">T
A
S
K</td><td>1.</td><td>View the installed printers. Do not change the printer settings.</td></tr>
<tr><td>2.</td><td>Close all applications.</td></tr>
</table>

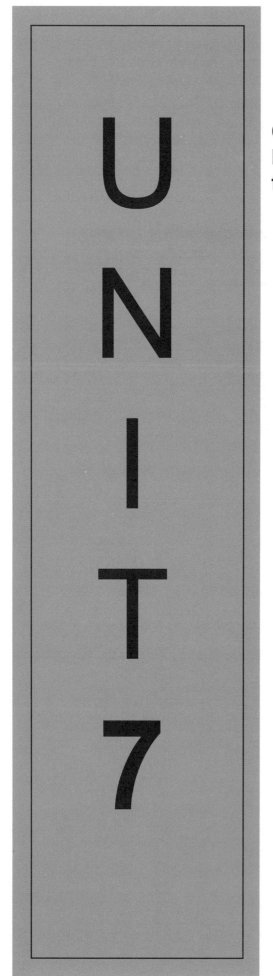

On completion of this unit you will have learnt about and practised the following:

GUI

Software Applications

- Spreadsheets
- Financial Applications
- Databases
- Word Processing
- Overwrite
- 'Read-only' Protection
- Presentation Graphics
- Desktop Publishing
- Computer-Aided Design

Integrated Applications

- Multi-tasking
- Mail Merge

GUI

Graphical User Interface or GUI is the method or process by which a user interacts with a technical device or object using graphics or images to operate that device.

In relation to computers, GUI takes the shape of buttons, drop lists, text field boxes, dialogue boxes and other controls utilised in order to interact with a program via a computer.

The GUI of a software application determines the 'look and feel' of that program and how 'user-friendly' or easy it may be for an end-user (you) to operate. The aesthetics of a program's graphical user interface are difficult to measure, as one programmer's notion as to what might be considered 'good' or 'right' may differ from that of another.

All Windows applications are based on GUIs.

Software Applications

Spreadsheets

Spreadsheets are widely used for financial planning, statistical analysis or simple day-to-day household expenditure.

The next few pages will recap the basics of Microsoft Excel. If you are confident with your knowledge, you can go straight onto the task at the end of this section.

To access **Excel**, click **Start**, **Programs**, **Microsoft Excel**.

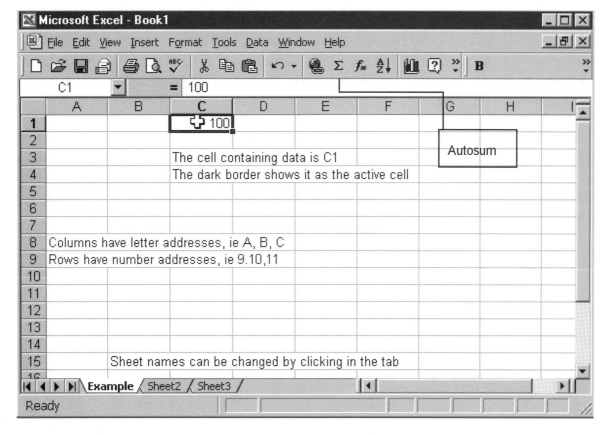

Formulae

Formulae are used to perform calculations on the data entered. Formulae consist of mathematical operators (**+** addition, ***** multiplication, **/** division, **-** subtraction), values and cell addresses where the cell contains a value to be used in the calculation. The formula is typed into the cell where the result of the calculation is required.

Examples of formulae:

=A1+A2   **=A1-A2**   **=A1/A2**   **=A1*A2**

A combination of the mathematical operators can be used, such as when calculating the average of values in cells:

=(B1+B2+B3)/3

Arithmetic follows the **BODMAS** rules of priority:

1.	Calculations enclosed in **brackets**	**B**
2.	Fractions (**of**)	**O**
3.	**Division**	**D**
4.	**Multiplication**	**M**
5.	**Addition**	**A**
6.	**Subtraction**	**S**

In the formula **=(B1+B2+B3)/3** the addition of cells **B1** to **B3** will be calculated first and the answer will then be divided by 3 to calculate the average. If the brackets were not used, the answer would be incorrect, as **B3** would be divided by 3 and the result of this would then be added to **B1+B2**.

Formulae can be entered into cells by typing directly into the required cell. Remember to use the '=' (equals) sign first. Alternatively, you can type the '=' sign and then select cells using the mouse, inserting the mathematical operators in-between cell references. If you decide that the formula is incorrect after starting to type it, press the **Esc** key on the keyboard to exit the cell. You can also edit directly into the cell by clicking or by pressing **F2.**

Functions

Functions are pre-defined worksheet formulae that enable you to do complex calculations easily. Like formulae, functions always begin with the = sign and you can enter them manually or you can use the Formula Palette. The most common functions used are **SUM**, **AVERAGE**, **MAX**, **MIN**, **COUNT**, **IF**. You can use the **Autosum** icon (shown overleaf) for simple **SUM** functions.

Formula Palette

An alternative way of creating a function is to use the **Formula Palette**. This displays the name and description of the function, each of its arguments, the current result of the function, and the current result of the entire formula.

Display the **Formula Palette** by clicking the **Edit Formula** button ▇ in the formula bar.

This will display the following:

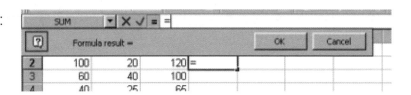

Select the function that you wish to use from the drop-down arrow.

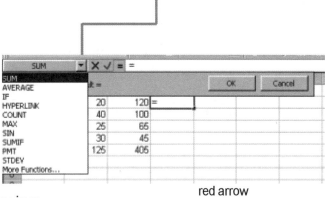

red arrow

The following dialogue box will be showing:

This shows which cells are currently being calculated.

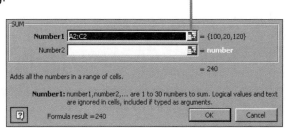

If the dialogue box is obscuring the view of the worksheet, click and hold the left mouse button on the grey area of the palette and drag to the required position and release the mouse button. Alternatively, click on the **red arrow** to toggle between full and partial view of the palette.

Check the cell references are correct and either click **OK** or press the **Enter** key.

If the cell references are incorrect, type in the correct cell references or highlight the correct range of cells to be calculated.

Inserting rows and columns

Additional rows and columns can be inserted into a worksheet by using the following method:

To insert additional columns, click the column where the new column is to be inserted. Select **Insert** from the menu bar. Click **Columns**.

For example, if an additional column was required in a workbook called **Expenses** between existing columns **A** and **B** (**Staff names** and **Monday**), column **B** would need to be selected. The new inserted column would now be column **B** (with **Monday** now becoming column **C**).

The whole worksheet is adjusted to accommodate the new column being inserted.

The same principle is applied to inserting additional rows, ie click to select the row where it is to be inserted. Select **Insert**, **Rows** from the menu bar.

The new row will appear **above** the rows that were selected, with all the other rows having then been readjusted.

Deleting rows and columns

When a column is deleted, the columns appearing to the right shift left to fill the space (readjust).

To **delete** a column(s), click to select it (or them), then select **Edit**, **Delete** from the menu bar.

When a row is deleted, the rows appearing below the deleted row move up to fill the space (readjust).

To delete a row(s), click to select it (or them), then select **Edit**, **Delete** from the menu bar.

T A S K

1. Open the spreadsheet application.

2. Open the file Datavision addresses located on the floppy disk.

3. A new address has been added. Enter the following data on a new row in the appropriate columns:

Mr Finnley
19 Barbery Drive
Tewbury
Lexton
Oxfordshire
LY3 9FG.

Gift Voucher	Prize
£150.00	DVD Player

<table>
<tr><td>T
A
S
K</td><td>

4. The price contained in the Gift Voucher column has been updated. The prices have been increased by 20%. Enter a formula that will calculate the difference and apply it to each price in the Gift Voucher column. Your formula will be similar to =150*1.2 (ie 120% of the price) or =150+150*20% (first price plus 20% of first price).

5. Insert a new column between Gift Voucher and Prize.

6. Print a copy of the spreadsheet document. Ensure it is printed on one sheet of A4 paper in Landscape orientation.

7. Create a new folder on your floppy disk called Prize Draw. Save the updated file as Datavision addresses v2 within the folder Prize Draw.

8. Close the document and close the spreadsheet application.

</td></tr>
</table>

Financial Applications

As well as Microsoft Excel, there are any number of business finance applications available on the market that will enable you to keep abreast of your business or personal expenses.

From investment software to accounting and inventory management, there are a wealth of financial applications with varying degrees of complexity, designed for all types of businesses.

A visit to **www.downloads.com** and selecting the **Business** option will provide access to both freeware and shareware business applications that can help keep your finances in order.

Databases

Access is different from Word or Excel in that you have to create a new database before you can add any tables.

The next few pages will recap the basics of Microsoft Access. If you are confident with your knowledge, you can go straight onto the task at the end of this section.

To start **Access**, click **Start**, **Programs**, **Microsoft Access**.

To create a new database, select **Blank Access database**. Click **OK**.

The **File New Database** dialogue will appear:

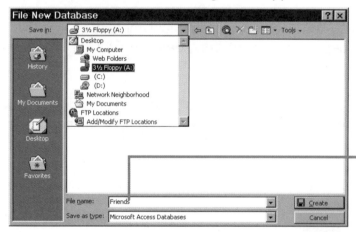

Select the location that you wish to save the file to from the **Save in:** drop-down arrow.

Type in a name for the new database in the **File name:** box.

Click **Create**.

A completely blank database will appear on your screen.

Creating a table

Tables contain data for the database. When you create a table you must define what data the table is to contain. The table has to be given its own name. The fields that the table contains have to be named and defined. To do this select **Create table in Design view**, then press the **Enter** key on the keyboard.

You would then create your table by adding field names and data types as appropriate.

Field name   **Data type**

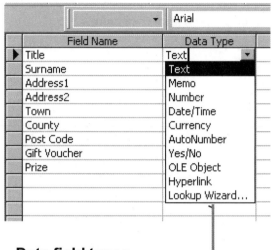

Field data types determine the kind of values that users can store in each field. Only one type of value can be used in a field at any one time.

Data field types

| T A S K | 1. | Create a new database called Datavision on your floppy disk. |
| | 2. | Create a new table using the field names and data types shown below. |

Field Names	Data Types
Title	Text
Surname	Text
Address1	Text
Address2	Text
Town	Text
County	Text
Post Code	Text
Gift Voucher	Currency
Prize	Text

3. Save the table as datavision. When asked if you wish to create a primary key, click No.

You are now going to use the Excel spreadsheet already created to import data into the Access database.

There are several ways to import an Excel spreadsheet into an Access database. If you have not already created your table, you can go to **File**, **Get External Data**, **Import**. You would then look on your disk for the Datavision addresses file (which must be closed) and follow the **Import Spreadsheet Wizard** with the final window selecting to import data into a new table.

However, for the purpose of this unit, you need to carry out the following method:

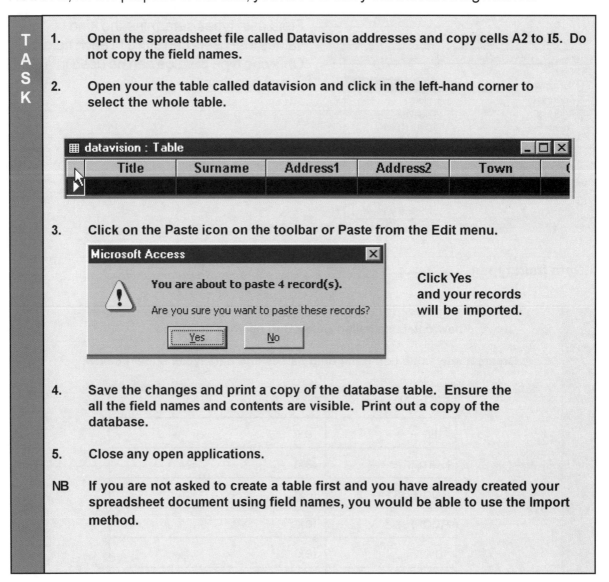

T A S K

1. Open the spreadsheet file called Datavison addresses and copy cells A2 to I5. Do not copy the field names.

2. Open your the table called datavision and click in the left-hand corner to select the whole table.

3. Click on the Paste icon on the toolbar or Paste from the Edit menu.

    Click Yes and your records will be imported.

4. Save the changes and print a copy of the database table. Ensure the all the field names and contents are visible. Print out a copy of the database.

5. Close any open applications.

NB If you are not asked to create a table first and you have already created your spreadsheet document using field names, you would be able to use the Import method.

Word Processing

Microsoft Word is quite possibly the most widely used application within the Microsoft Office software package.

Word processing is used for documents such as reports, letters, business plans etc.

Together with the other Microsoft applications in Office, the word processing application provides the user with the opportunity of streamlining the process of creating, sharing, reviewing and publishing their documents. The next few pages will recap the basics of Microsoft Word. If you are confident with your knowledge, you can go straight to the task at the end of this section.

To access **Word**, click **Start**, **Programs**, **Microsoft Word**.

Working with Word

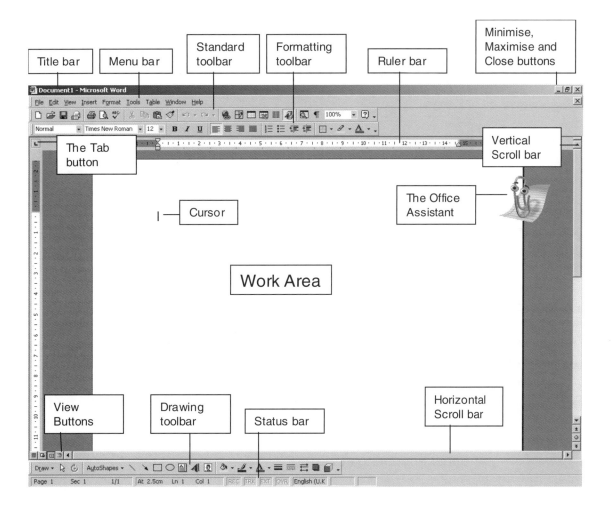

Page setup

When producing documents, it is important to consider their presentation, ie how the document will look with respect to orientation, paper size, margin widths etc. To set this type of criteria for a document **Page Setup** is used. The **Page Setup** dialogue box will allow a document to be adjusted.

Select **File**, **Page Setup** from the menu bar and the **Page Setup** dialogue box will be displayed.

Ensure that the **Paper Size** tab is selected:

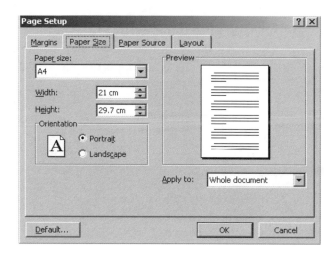

To change the paper size, click on the drop-down arrow and select the size required. The dialogue box contains a **Preview** pane. When applying any settings, check that the preview looks correct before clicking **OK**.

Page orientation

Orientation is the way in which the document will be displayed on the paper, there are two ways which are:

Portrait   -   Documents in portrait format will have the short edge of the paper appearing at the top.

Landscape   -   Documents in landscape format will have the short edge of the paper appearing at the top.

Margins

Margins are the space between the edge of the text and the edge of the paper. In word processing, the size of each margin can be controlled. Imagine a document with no margin area. When printed, the document text would appear too close or even over the edge of the paper. It is for this reason that a margin area is set, giving a neat edge or frame around the page. There are four margins, **Top**, **Bottom**, **Left** and **Right**.

To adjust margins, select **File**, **Page Setup** and select the **Margins** tab.

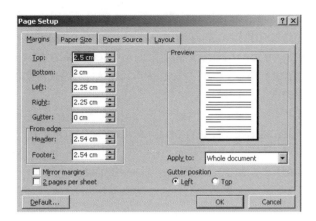

Notice the existing margin settings together with a preview pane. Each time a margin setting is changed the preview will be updated.

New measurements can be set by clicking on the upper or lower arrows appearing next to the measurement. As they are clicked the measurement will change. Using this method will increase or decrease the measurement in 10ths of a centimetre (cm). For a more accurate measurement, double-click in the box and type in the new measurement.

Enhancement

Attributes such as **Bold**, <u>Underline</u> and *Italic* can be applied using the Formatting toolbar. After selecting the text, click on a button to apply. This is often known as text enhancement. Here are some examples:

The buttons act in a similar way to an 'on' and 'off' switch, ie to activate or switch the bold attribute on, highlight/select the text and click on the **Bold** button on the toolbar. To remove bold, highlight/select the text and click again on the **Bold** button.

Spelling and grammar

All documents should be checked for spelling errors. Each word in your document is checked against a standard dictionary. If a word is unknown to the dictionary it will be 'flagged' by the appearance of a red wavy line underneath the word (if this feature is activated on your computer). You can choose to either check the whole document or a selection which has been highlighted.

Click the **Spelling and Grammar** button on the Standard toolbar.

The **Spelling and Grammar** dialogue box will be displayed.

The **Not in Dictionary** box displays the unrecognised word in red together with a suggestion in the box below.

One of the buttons on the right must be selected before the checker can move onto the next word within the document.

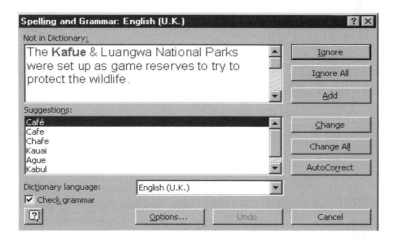

Ignore	-	Skips the highlighted word without making changes
Ignore All	-	Skips over all occurrences of the word, throughout this document only, without making changes
Add	-	Adds the highlighted word to the dictionary on the computer
Change	-	Replaces the original word with a chosen suggestion
Change All	-	Replaces all occurrences of the word, throughout this document only, with a chosen suggestion
AutoCorrect	-	Adds a misspelled word and its correction to the AutoCorrect list, future misspelling of the word will be automatically corrected

The spell checker may not recognise the names of people or places. If they are used regularly, check them manually and add them to the dictionary.

Click **OK** when the spelling and grammar check is complete.

Overwrite

Sometimes you may want to replace a Word file with a new or changed file. To protect work that has already been produced, Word will display a warning sign that lets you know that you are attempting to replace an existing document. This is often referred to as **overwriting** a document. The message that would be displayed is shown below.

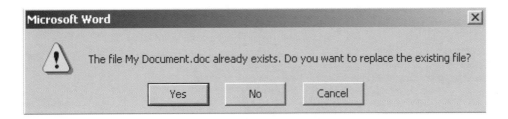

'Read-only' Protection

As you create documents, you may want to protect them from other users' interference. This may be particularly useful if your document has taken a lot of time and effort and you don't want it altered in any way. To safeguard against this, you can make the document 'Read-only'. This means that any other user can only access the document to view the contents, and will not be able to save any changes they might make. This protection process is carried out in Windows Explorer.

Select the File you want to protect and right click it, select **Properties** from the list. Select the **General** tab. In the **Attributes** section, check the **Read-only** box and click **Apply**. This will protect the document and prevent any
other users from changing the contents.

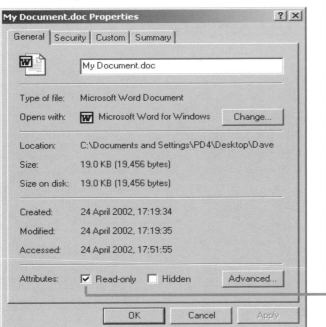

However, it is important to remember that unless the document is password protected, another user could remove the Read-only attribute and then make changes to your document.

Presentation Graphics

Presentation Graphics is the software that allows you to create, organise and design effective presentations, either by printing onto overhead transparencies, producing 35mm slides or by running the software as an automated slide show on the PC screen or through a projector. Microsoft PowerPoint and Lotus Freelance are examples of Presentation Graphics software.

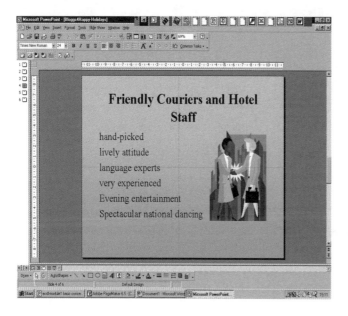

An example of a slide from a Microsoft PowerPoint presentation

Desktop Publishing

Desktop Publishing (**DTP**) is the software that allows you to create professional looking manuals and brochures. Whilst word processors can perform most of the DTP functions, large publishing houses use dedicated DTP packages. Microsoft Publisher and Adobe PageMaker are examples of Desktop Publishing software.

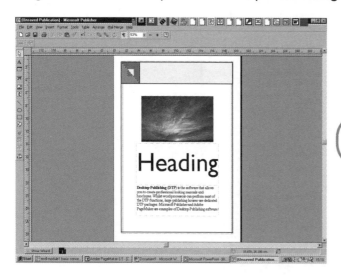

An example of a Microsoft Publisher document

Computer Aided Design

Computer Aided Design (CAD) is the use of computers to assist the design process. It is often used in industry to design complex machinery and also in architecture when drawing up plans for large structures. Specialised CAD programs exist for various types of design: architecture, electronics, engineering electronics, roadways and woven fabrics to name but a few.

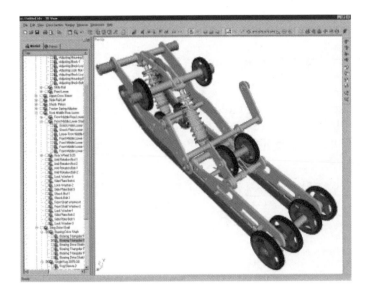

This image shows example of a Computer-Aided Design. There are many different types of software on the market that allow you to design complex structures such as this.

Integrated Applications

Multi-tasking

Integrated software packages contain a number of different programs that enable the user to open more than one software application within a single operating system. This is known as multi-tasking.

Lotus Smartsuite, Sage Financial Solutions and Microsoft Office are three software packages that have been designed to offer users a complete solution based on their particular needs.

For all your office and administration needs, there are few better integrated software applications on the market than Microsoft Office. The great advantage of any multi-tasking operating system (such as Windows) is the ease with which text, graphics, tables, photographic imagery etc, can be inserted from one software application to the next. Incorporated within the design of the GUI (Graphical User Interface) of each application are links to all the other applications within the package. This eliminates the need to save your work in a particular format in order for it to be inserted into another software application.

Of the many software applications that comprise the Microsoft Office software package, Word, Excel and Access are possibly the most widely used.

Mail Merge

You can use Mail Merge to create letters, mailing labels, envelopes or catalogues. The Mail Merge guides you through organising data and merging it into a generic document.

New or existing documents can be used for Mail Merge. The 'data source' can be created using the mail merge helper or existing data can be used from database or spreadsheet files.

T A S K

1. **Open your Word Processing application.**

2. **Open the file Datavision Productions document from the floppy disk. This is the main document.**

3. **You are required to insert the spreadsheet file called Datavision addresses onto a new page. Place your cursor at the end of the document and click Insert, Break, choose the option Next Page as shown.**

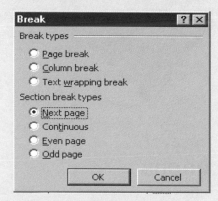

   Place your cursor in the new page, click Insert, File and change the option Files of Type to show All Files. Double-click on the Datavision addresses file to import it. You may wish to format the spreadsheet table to fit the page.

4. **Move your cursor onto page 1.**

5. **You are now required to use the Mail Merge facility. Select Tools, Mail Merge.**

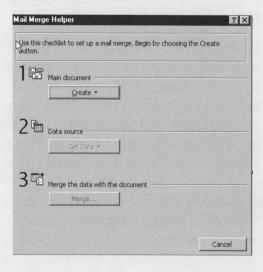

T A S K

You now need to set up the main document to add the appropriate fields and find the data source which will be used for the merge.

6. Click Create, Form Letters and choose the Active Window. This is because your text has already been created for you.

7. Next, you need to find your data source. Click Get Data and Open Data Source. You will need to change the type of files so that all files can be seen. From your disk, choose the database file called dvd. There is only one table in the database, so select that. Next, you will need to set up the main document. Choose Edit Main Document.

8. Place the cursor where you want to start typing the first line of the address and click on the Insert Merge Field button from the Merge toolbar that has appeared.

You will see a drop-down menu of all fields in your data source file.

The fields should be inserted as follows:

«Title»«Surname»
«Address1»
«Address2»
«Town»
«County»
«Post_Code»

Dear«Title»«Surname»,

9. Before merging the documents, apply bold styling, italics and increase font sizing to the letter where you think appropriate.

10. Apply the spell check to the whole document and proofread for any other errors.

11. Select Tools, Mail Merge, Merge to merge the documents.

12. Check the printer settings for economy mode (if available) and print out each merged letter.

13. Save the merged file as Prize Draw onto your floppy disk.

14. Close Word and any other open applications (do not save the changes to any other documents).

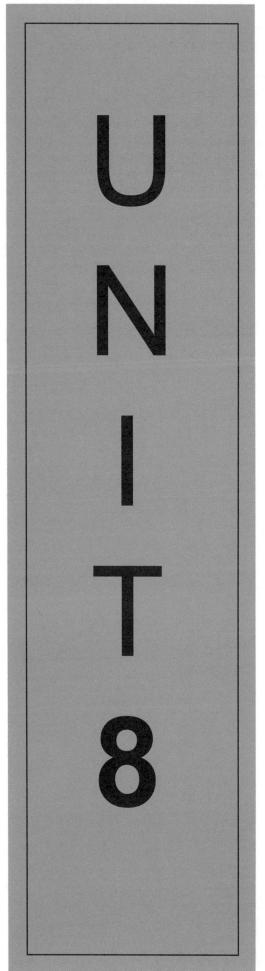

On completion of this unit you will have learnt about and practised the following:

The Internet

- Hardware
- Dial-up Networking
- Software
- Dial-up Connection
- Downloading
- Freeware And Shareware
- Public Domain

Using E-mail

Protecting Your Work

- Licensing And Multi-licensing
- Software Copyright
- Data Protection Act
- Data Corruption

Computer Graphics

- Bitmap Graphics
- Vector-based Graphics
- Photographic Images

The Internet

Hardware

Before you can access the Web, you need to be connected to the Internet. There are generally three main options for gaining access to the Internet: The company you work for or the college you are with may provide direct access. A cybercafe or public library is another option. However, the most common method is to use a modem to connect to the Internet yourself.

Essentially, you need the following components to establish a dial-up connection.

Computer

Generally, as a minimum requirement, you will need a computer with a 66MHz processor, 16Mb of RAM and 50-150Mb of free hard-disk space. A faster, more powerful computer with more RAM will make browsing the Internet quicker, and ultimately more enjoyable.

Modem

There are two types of modem: internal (one that's fitted into your computer) and external (a modem that's attached as an addition to your computer). Modems come in a variety of speeds, with 56kbps being the most common.

Internet Service Provider (ISP)

A service provider has a computer system that is permanently connected to the Internet and to a 'bank' of modems. When connecting to the Internet, you use your modem to connect to one of your service provider's modems via your telephone line, thereby making your computer (temporarily) part of the Internet.

Telephone line

Most ISPs offer connection at local rates. It is always a good idea to check, to avoid running up a huge telephone bill.

Connection software

On your own PC you will need to run 'install the Dial-Up Networking' facility supplied with Windows to connect to the Internet hardware.

For your information only

Dial-up Networking

Depending on your operating system, you have two methods of setting up the dial-up networking program.

In Windows 2000, the Dial-up Networking option is on the **Start, Settings** drop-down menu. In Windows 98, you will find the icon by double-clicking on **My Computer.** Whichever option you choose, a window will open, asking you to make a new connection.

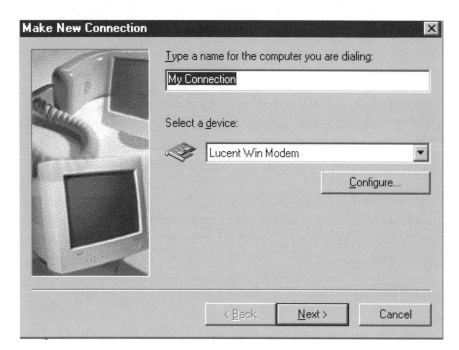

If you are using several Service Providers, give each one a name that will remind you of the dial up.

If you have several devices connected to your computer, use the drop-down menu to select the appropriate one.

Follow the wizard, entering the appropriate telephone number and when completed, open the connection to fill in your user name and password details as shown below:

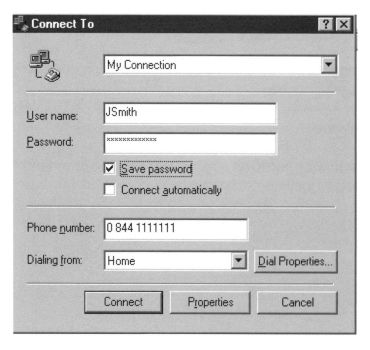

The following components (overleaf) are also needed to explore the Internet.

Software

You will need a software application known as a **web browser**. A browser enables you to find web pages and display them on your screen. There are several types of web browser software available, the most popular being **Microsoft's Internet Explorer** and **Netscape Navigator**.

Dial-up Connection

Once you have installed Internet Explorer on your computer, you are now ready to access the Internet via your ISP (Internet Service Provider). The Dial-up connection software should be incorporated with the web browser. However, if you have already set up your Dial-up connection, you will not need to do this again.

As soon as you open Internet Explorer, it will attempt to connect to the Internet. If the computer you are using is part of a network or has a permanent Internet connection, then Internet Explorer will do this automatically.

If the computer you are using is not part of a network or does not have a permanent Internet connection, then you might see the following screen:

This is your dial-up connection screen and it will contain the name/password details of your Internet Service Provider (ISP). You do have the options of changing the name/ password or ISP from this screen, but usually you will just have to press the **Connect** button to continue. When you've done this, your computer will attempt to connect to your ISP and if this is successful, then you will be connected to the Internet.

When you've connected to the Internet, your web browser will automatically display the browser's **home page**. This home page can be modified to suit your own needs at a later stage.

Downloading

It's possible to download lots of files from the Internet, including demo versions of commercial software and plug-ins that can enhance the performance of your web browser.

With some files (usually TV and radio transmissions), a process called streaming is sometimes used. This method allows you to listen to or watch a sound or video file while it is actually downloading. This can help to save time, especially if the file is quite large.

Streaming formats, however, cannot compete with saving sound or video files to your hard drive. A lot of information has to be omitted in order for you to download and play a file simultaneously.

Ideally, you will almost always want to save your downloads to the hard drive. You will then be able to experiment with the download once you have logged off the Internet.

If you're looking for downloads, there are few better sites on the Internet than www.downloads.com . This site has downloads for a host of different software.

NB Do not download any software onto machines within the college, university or workplace without prior agreement. An example screen from the **www.downloads.com** site is shown below.

> At the head of the list of downloads, you will find details of how many downloads are available and the number of pages they are contained on. Obviously you are not required to scroll through each page, but do have a look at a number of the items available before making a selection.

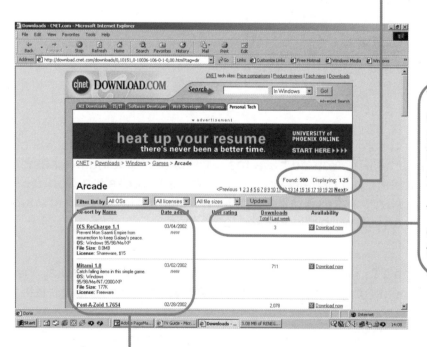

> To the right you have details of the software's popularity, how often it has been downloaded and its availability.
>
> You are also given the option of downloading the software.

> The column to the left gives you the name of the download, together with a brief description. Also listed is the file size of the software program.

NB **The following task will require that you download an item from the Internet from a specific location.**

T
A
S
K

1. **Type the URL http://download.tektra-connect.co.uk in the address toolbar of your browser.**

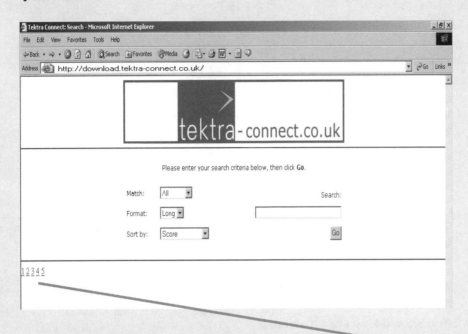

2. **From the tektra-connect.co.uk web page pictured above, select the numbers to view the available items for download. Alternatively, type in the item you wish to download in the Search box and click Go.**

3. **Find the Access file.**

4. **Click on the file name to read specific information about the selected file.**

5. **Follow the on-screen instructions to download the file.**

6. **The web browser you are using will then ask whether you would like to run the file from its current location, or save it to a specified location. Select Save this file to disk and click OK.**

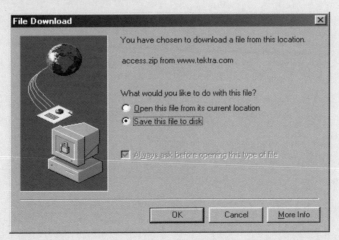

NB **At this point, you may have to wait a few seconds before you are prompted to save your download.**

Continued over the page...

T
A
S
K

7. The Save As dialogue box will appear allowing you to specify where you wish to save the file. Click the drop-down menu and select the 3½ floppy (A:).

NB When downloading files the normal location to save them would be on the C: drive.

8. The dialogue box pictured below will then appear, illustrating the various files belonging to the download being copied from the Internet to your computer.

You should also see an estimate of the time it will take for the file to be downloaded.

The dialogue box will close automatically on completion if a tick has been placed in the box

9. Close the Internet browser and find the downloaded file in the location that you specified.

You can continue to surf the Internet while your software is downloading. The dialogue box can be minimised to the taskbar at the foot of your screen, where you can keep an eye on how your download is progressing.

Once your software has been successfully downloaded, double-click the file to open or run. Follow instructions, if available, for running software (if appropriate) - these will differ from one download to the next.

Freeware And Shareware

While downloading from the Internet, you may have noticed the terms **freeware** and **shareware** in relation to the license of the software. This is present in the description section of the software application.

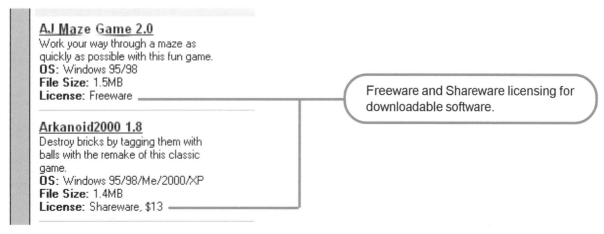

AJ Maze Game 2.0
Work your way through a maze as quickly as possible with this fun game.
OS: Windows 95/98
File Size: 1.5MB
License: Freeware

Arkanoid2000 1.8
Destroy bricks by tagging them with balls with the remake of this classic game.
OS: Windows 95/98/Me/2000/XP
File Size: 1.4MB
License: Shareware, $13

Freeware and Shareware licensing for downloadable software.

Freeware

Freeware is software you can download, pass around and distribute without payment. However, it's still copyrighted, so you can't change it or sell it on as your own software.

Shareware

Like freeware, shareware is available from centralized archives on the Internet (or sometimes via CD-ROM or floppy). Shareware is copyrighted but works on the honour system. You have a specified time period (usually a month) to try out the software for free. If you continue to use it, you're expected to register the programme and pay a fee to its developer. (Some programs are partially disabled, meaning they have been programmed to stop working after a set period of time, or contain 'nag screens' that pop up frequently to encourage you to register.)

Registration fees can vary and some selfless developers ask only that you send an e-mail letting them know you like their product. Registering often gets you full documentation or free software updates.

Public Domain

Of all the kinds of software or information you can download, public domain has the least strings attached. With shareware, you're expected to pay a fee. With freeware, you may face other restrictions, such as the software only being a limited version of the original, and there's still a copyright attached. With public domain downloads (also called downloads in the public domain), there are no copyright restrictions whatsoever.

Using E-mail

Essentially, e-mail is the electronic equivalent of sending letters and faxes. Whether the recipient happens to be down the road, in another city or in another country, sending an e-mail is equally fast, and costs the same price for any destination. Another great advantage of using e-mail is the ability to attach other documents to the e-mail message. This means that documents, pictures, sound samples and program files can accompany your message.

When you send an e-mail message it is delivered to the recipient's Internet Service Provider, usually within a couple of minutes. It is stored in the recipient's mailbox until he or she next logs on and checks for new mail.

The illustrations in this section are taken from Outlook.

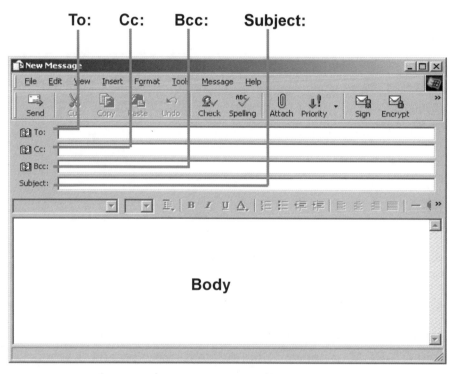

When sending an e-mail, there is a header section to every message that contains the following details:

To:	In this space, you enter the e-mail address of the person you want to communicate with. This person is normally called the recipient. Ensure you enter the correct e-mail address, otherwise you will receive an error message saying the address has not been found.
Cc:	There may be recipients who you want to copy the message to. This is the space used for the **Carbon copy**.
Bcc:	Other recipients of the message will not see the name of the recipient in the **Blind carbon copy** text area.
Subject:	The heading or title of the message is entered here. It is useful as it helps identify the mail you are searching for. The more accurate the subject, the easier it is to find again. The recipient may ignore the e-mail message if you do not specify the contents. If there is a reply to the e-mail, the response will be titled **Re: [Whatever the original subject title was]** (eg **Re: Welcome**).
Body:	The main body of the e-mail contains the message itself.

Open Attached files

E-mail sent with an attachment will arrive in the inbox with a small **paperclip icon** to the left of the message, under the paperclip column.

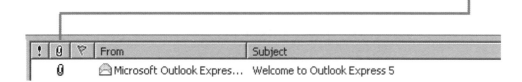

To view an attachment that happens to be a picture, use the scroll bar in the preview pane (the picture will be located at the bottom of the e-mail), or double-click the e-mail subject title to open the message in a separate window.

If the attachment in question is a document, open the message in a separate window. The header details will contain an **Attach** section, showing the file type and size of the attachment(s). Double-click the **attachment icon** to open it.

Save Attachment Files

If you have an e-mail message with an attachment, it is possible to save the attachment separately. Access Outlook Express and open an e-mail from your inbox that has an attachment. If you double-click the e-mail so that it appears in its own window, the attachment(s) will be contained in the heading section:

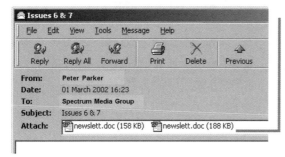

Double-click on attachment to open the file and save it by selecting **File**, **Save As**. Choose an appropriate name and location.

Alternatively, select the message with attachment, so that it appears in the lower window pane.

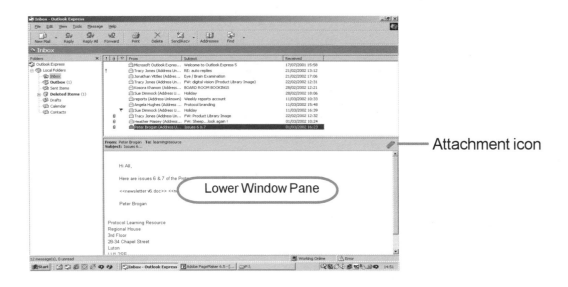

Attachment icon

Lower Window Pane

Click the attachment icon to activate a menu containing the attachment(s). Select **Save Attachments...**

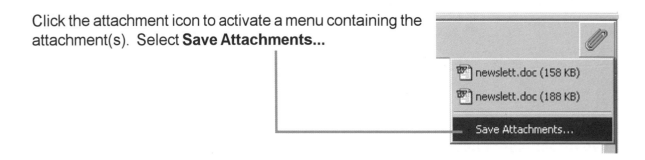

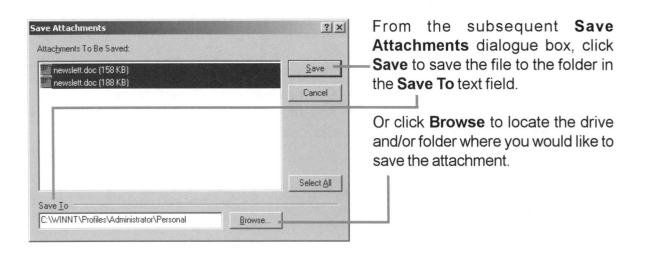

From the subsequent **Save Attachments** dialogue box, click **Save** to save the file to the folder in the **Save To** text field.

Or click **Browse** to locate the drive and/or folder where you would like to save the attachment.

Protecting Your Work

Licensing And Multi-licensing

Software licensing exempts software publishers from all liability under consumer protection law. Not only does the 'purchaser' have no rights, there are no requirements placed on the publisher, nor is there any requirement that a program even works.

What you actually get for your money is the privilege (not right) to use a software package in accordance with the conditions of the license. That privilege may be revoked by the publisher at any time, with or without cause.

Using Microsoft as an example, as their products are the most widely used, their software licenses are 'non-concurrent'. In other words, if you have 9 computers that run Office, but no more than 4 ever run Office at the same time, you still need to buy 9 licenses.

Software Copyright

Under the 1988 Copyright Designs and Patents Act, computer programs are now protected as literary works. Databases may receive copyright protection for the selection and arrangement of their contents. This is an automatic right and protects databases against the unauthorised extraction and re-utilisation of the contents of the database. Database rights last for 15 years from their making but, if published during this time, then the term is 15 years from publication.

Copyright law gives the creators of literary, dramatic, musical, artistic works, sound recordings, broadcasts, films and typographical arrangement of published editions the right to control the ways in which their material may be used.

Data Protection Act

In processing personal information, data users, in accordance with the 1998 Data Protection Act, must have regard to and comply with the eight enforceable principles of good practice:

- fairly and lawfully processed
- processed for limited purposes
- adequate, relevant and not excessive
- accurate
- not kept longer than necessary
- processed in accordance with the data subject's rights
- secure
- not transferred to countries without adequate protection

Personal data covers both facts and opinions about the individual. It also includes information regarding the intentions of the data controller towards the individual, although in some limited circumstances, exemptions will apply. With processing, the definition is far wider than before. For example, it incorporates the concepts of 'obtaining', 'holding' and 'disclosing'.

Data Corruption

Although data corruption comes in many forms, the most common is when information contained in a data file contains 'non-standard' characters. The presence of non-standard characters often prevents software from being able to work with the data properly. This is because the software cannot read the data and/or cannot write over the corrupted data with new information.

So what is the best defence against data corruption?

Try to connect your computer, monitor, printer, modem, and other peripheral devices to an Uninterruptable Power Supply (UPS). A UPS will protect the computer against:

*   Power blackouts (no power)
*   Power brownouts (reduced power)
*   Surges (increased power)
*   Spikes (massive increases in power, eg lightning)
*   Electromagnetic Radio Interference (EMI) (caused by, among other things, sunspots)
*   Radio Frequency Interference (RFI)

An Uninterruptable Power Supply is a cheap insurance policy and will significantly extend the life of your computer equipment.

NB   Don't connect laser printers to a UPS as they require too much power and the UPS won't be able to handle it.

Backup the files on your computer at least once a week, and rotate the media (floppy disks, zip disks, CD-RW, etc) on which you backup. Store your backup files in a cool, dry storage facility away from excessive heat, light or moisture.

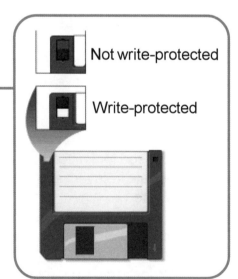

Protection against erasing and recording information on a floppy disk. You can write-protect a 3.5 inch floppy disk by moving a little plastic tab to the write-protected position.

Not write-protected

Write-protected

Run anti-virus software in auto-protect mode. Some popular and effective anti-virus software programs include: *McAfee Anti-Virus*, *Norton Anti-Virus*, and *Dr. Solomon Anti-Virus*. Shareware versions of many anti-virus software applications are available via the Internet.

Regularly run the reindex (aka 'rebuild') maintenance functions contained in your software. This can also help prevent the loss or corruption of data.

Computer Graphics

Bitmap Graphics

Bitmap graphics (also called "raster") are created from rows of different coloured pixels that together form an image. In their simplest form, bitmaps have only two colours, with each pixel being either black or white. With increasing complexity, an image can include more colours; photographic-quality images may have millions. Examples of bitmap graphic formats include GIF, JPEG, PNG, TIFF, XBM, MacPaint, BMP and PCX as well as bitmap ('screen') fonts. The image displayed on a computer monitor is also a bitmap, as are the outputs of printers, scanners and similar devices. They are created using photographic manipulation programmes like Adobe Photoshop.

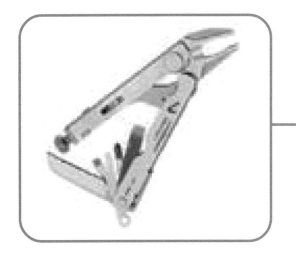

Bitmap images can contain a wide spectrum of colours, but their resolution can become diffused when the image is enlarged.

Vector-based Graphics

Vector (also known as 'object-oriented') graphics are constructed using mathematical formulas describing shapes, colours and placement. Rather than a grid of pixels, a vector graphic consists of shapes, curves, lines and text which together make a picture.

While a bitmap image contains information about the colour of each pixel, a vector graphic contains instructions about where to place each of the components. Examples of vector graphic formats include PICT, EPS and WMF, as well as PostScript and TrueType fonts. They are created with Geographic Information Systems (GIS) and Computer-Aided Design (CAD) applications as well as drawing programmes like Freehand and Corel Draw.

A vector-based image does not contain a wide variation in terms of colour, but will not lose any detail in resolution once enlarged.

Bitmap and vector graphics both have their strengths and weaknesses:

- In general, a bitmap graphic is much larger than a similar vector graphic. Bitmap graphics are resolution-dependent. If you enlarge a bitmap graphic, it will look jagged. When shrunk, its features can become indistinct and fuzzy. This does not happen with vector graphics, as their shapes are redrawn to compensate for changes in resolution.

- Altering vector graphics is easy because the shapes within them can be ungrouped and edited individually. However, vector graphics are difficult to modify or even display when they are not opened in programs that understand their rendering languages. Most paint applications, however, are capable of opening many different kinds of bitmap graphic formats.

- It is fairly easy to convert one kind of bitmap file into another. It is usually possible to convert a vector graphic into a bitmap. However, while it is sometimes possible to embed a bitmap image as an object within a vector graphic, it is very difficult to convert a bitmap graphic into a true vector graphic. It is even difficult to convert one kind of vector graphic into another (eg PICT to WMF).

- Vector graphics are not appropriate for complex images (eg digitised photographic images).

Photographic Images

Photographic images are often used in computer-processed documents. You may have already come across several in this resource pack. Photographs can be downloaded off the Internet, although there will be copyright restrictions on many images. Another popular way of manipulating photographic images is through a scanner or by using a digital camera. This is becoming a favourite method of storing images on a PC. Here is an example of a photographic image. As you can see, the image is of extremely high quality.

T A S K	On your floppy disk there are 3 files called beach. One is a jpg file, one is a gif file and one is a bmp file.

On your floppy disk there are 3 files called beach. One is a jpg file, one is a gif file and one is a bmp file.

1. Look at the size of each file to compare them. You will notice there is a considerable difference between the jpg file and the bmp. This is an important fact to consider if you are creating reports or presentations using many imported pictures.

   Usually in the Microsoft Office suite of programs there is an application in Microsoft Office Tools called Photo Editor. This program enables you to open files of one image type and Save As another.

2. Find a picture on the Internet and Save As different file formats.

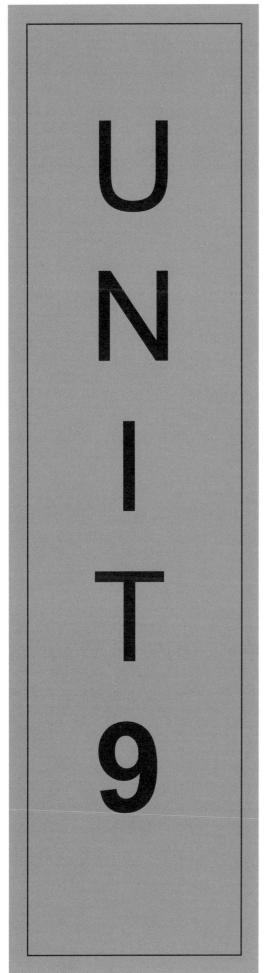

On completion of this unit you will have learnt about and practised:

Health And Safety

- Health And Safety Procedures
- Ergonomics
- Cleaning Computer Components
- A Safe And Comfortable Work Environment
- Repetitive Strain Injury
- Identifying Hazards

Health And Safety

Health And Safety Procedures

Your health and safety welfare at work is protected by law. Your employer has a duty to protect you and keep you informed about health and safety issues. If there is a problem, discuss it with your employer or safety representative (if there is one). **The Health and Safety Executive (HSE) are there to ensure that risks to your health and safety from work activities are properly controlled.**

In general, your employer's duties include:

- making your workplace safe and without risks to health

- ensuring plant, machinery, electrical equipment etc are safe and that systems at work are set out and followed correctly

- providing adequate welfare facilities

- giving you the information, instruction, training and supervision necessary for your health and safety

Ergonomics

In its most simplistic form, ergonomics is concerned with the interaction of humans and objects and how these objects can be created so that they are of maximum benefit to the user.

The application of ergonomics ranges from the design of a toothbrush to the layout of aircraft cockpits, from the design of baby carriages to wholesale packaging. Within the office environment, it is important that well-designed office equipment and furniture is used to gain maximum efficiency from employees, while ensuring they are both safe and comfortable. Chairs giving good back and leg support are essential if employees are in a sitting position for most of their working day. Sit back and in an upright position so that your lower back is fully supported by the chair and the soles of your feet are both firmly on the ground.

Computer screens/monitors should be positioned at arm's length from the user, ensuring the top of the monitor is at eye level. The screen display should be flicker-free and there should be gentle lighting that does not produce a glare on the screen. If the lighting is natural, ie through a nearby window, blinds can be used to minimise the light.

Ideally, wrist supports should be used and the keyboard should not be placed near to the edge of the desk.

Cleaning Computer Components

Cleaning your computer and your computer components helps keep them in good working condition. The environment that your computer operates in determines how often you should clean your computer.

If the location in which the computer is occupied is a non-smoking environment, it is recommended you clean your computer components every five months as well as doing the standard dusting.

If you are an end-user who smokes in the location of the computer, it is recommend that you clean your computer components every three months as well as doing the standard dusting.

System unit

The plastic case, ie the system unit that houses the PC components, can be cleaned with a lint-free cloth that has been slightly dampened with water. For stubborn stains, add a little household detergent to the cloth. It is recommended that you never use a solvent cleaner on plastic.

CD-ROM drive

A dirty CD-ROM drive can cause read errors with CD discs, preventing you from installing software or causing errors during the installation of software.

To clean the CD-ROM drive it is recommended that you purchase a CD-ROM cleaner, available from any reputable electrical retailer. Using a CD-ROM cleaner should suffi- ciently clean the CD-ROM laser of dust, dirt and hair.

Compact disks

Cleaning **CDs** can be done with a CD cleaning kit, but it can also be done with a normal clean cotton cloth or shirt. When using a clean cotton cloth or shirt, wipe against the tracks, starting from the middle of the CD and wiping towards the outer side of the CD. Never wipe with the tracks; doing so may add more scratches to the CD.

It is recommended that when cleaning a CD, water be used. However, if the substance on a CD cannot be removed using water, pure alcohol can also be used.

Floppy disks

Dirty read/write heads on the floppy disk drive can cause errors during the reading and/ or writing process.

The recommended method of cleaning a floppy drive is to purchase a kit at your local retail store designed to clean the read/write heads on your floppy drive.

Hard drive

While hard drives cannot be cleaned physically they can be cleaned with various utilities on the computer to help it run faster and more efficiently. Utilising these utilities will prevent the hard drive slowing down.

Running system software programs such as Scandisk and Defrag will help to delete unwanted files that take up unnecessary space on the hard drive.

Keyboard

If the keyboard has anything spilt into it, not taking the proper steps can cause the keyboard to be destroyed.

Many people clean the keyboard by turning it upside down and shaking. A more effective method is to use compressed air. Compressed air is pressurized air contained in a can with a very long nozzle. Simply aim the air between the keys and blow away all of the dust and debris that has gathered there.

A vacuum cleaner can also be used, but make sure the keyboard does not have loose keys that could possibly be sucked up by the vacuum cleaner.

The monitor

The monitor screen can be cleaned with ordinary household glass cleaner. As with all components that are to be cleaned, ensure the monitor is not switched on.

Remove dirt from the monitor by spraying cleaner onto a lint-free cloth and applying it evenly over the face of the screen. Vacuum off any dust that has settled on top of the monitor, and make sure objects have not been placed over the air vents. Obstructed monitor vents can cause the monitor to overheat or even catch on fire.

Mouse

A dirty optical-mechanical mouse can cause the on-screen mouse point to be difficult to control.

A Safe And Comfortable Work Environment

Adequate ventilation and an even room temperature (approximately 16°C) are important factors in creating a productive working environment. It is also important to keep all computer equipment in a safe and clean condition; power cables should be sound and stored securely so they cannot be tripped over. Power sockets must be fused, in good working order and not overloaded.

Cleaning the screen with a light non-static cloth and an electronically tested cleaning agent (preferably dispensed through an aerosol device), while keeping the computer and all peripherals free from the build-up of dust, will help maintain the computer in correct working order.

Repetitive Strain Injury

It is imperative that eyes are rested periodically by looking away from the screen and focusing on distant objects. To avoid fatigue, a short break away from the computer should be taken every hour.

Strain on the eyes, fatigue and headaches can be reduced by performing these simple tasks, together with the prevention of muscle strains in the neck and the shoulders. Repetitive Strain Injury (RSI) is caused by the prolonged and continuous use of particular muscles, and can affect many parts of the body. Periodically interrupting the posture adopted while using the computer can prevent the onset of RSI.

Identifying Hazards

In the event of a potential hazard in the workplace being identified, such as loose computer cables or the accumulation of discarded equipment obstructing a gangway, this should be reported immediately to a senior staff member so that the danger can be countered.

This Page is

intentionally

Left Blank

This Page is

intentionally

Left Blank

This Page is

intentionally

Left Blank